Engaging Heaven for Revelation

Volume 1

Receiving Riches from Heaven

Deb,
May you
live from
Revelation!

by

Dr. Ron M. Horner

Ron

Engaging Heaven for Revelation

Volume 1

Receiving Riches from Heaven

By

Dr. Ron M. Horner

www.CourtsOfHeaven.Net
PO Box 2167
Albemarle, North Carolina 28002

Engaging Heaven for Revelation – Volume 1

Receiving Riches from Heaven

Requests for bulk sales discounts, editorial permissions, or other information should be addressed to:

LifeSpring Publishing
PO Box 2167
Albemarle, NC 28002 USA

Additional copies available at www.courtsofheaven.net

ISBN 13 TP: 978-1-953684-06-6
ISBN 13 eBook: 978-1-953684-07-3

Cover Design by Darian Horner Design
(www.darianhorner.com)
Image: 123rf.com #117071279

First Edition: January 2021

10 9 8 7 6 5 4 3 2 1

Printed in the United States of America

Table of Contents

Acknowledgements

With much gratitude I want to recognize the ongoing work of Donna Neeper, my Executive Assistant. She is uniquely graced to engage Heaven and hear what Heaven is saying. Thank you to my daughters Bethany and Darian for their editorial assistance on this book. Thanks to the awesome Courts of Heaven team who work tirelessly to see people brought to freedom through the Courts of Heaven and engagements with Heaven. Thanks also to my audience and supporters. May the blessings of Heaven overflow in your life.

Foreword

In early 2011, I was seeking the Lord on how to enter the realms of Heaven and to see the real life beyond this earthly realm. The Lord directed me to study Colossians 3: verses 1-3. That started my journey. Dr. Ron Horner entered that realm and has written on it in so much detail that you will feel like you can enter there yourself—so it is, and so you can.

Following the deep illumination given in this book, *Engaging Heaven for Revelation*, you will see and understand the activities of the heavenlies and glimpse into the many dimensions and places of divine life that await us.

Dr. Ron reveals the "manifold wisdom of God being made known by the church" with chapters such as "Plundering the Enemy's Camp," "Dealing with Hope Deferred" and "Understanding Realms." This book will help you to better activate the angelic realm and all the spiritual beings that are assigned to co-labor with you in your walk in the heavenlies.

When Jesus ascended, we ascended *in* Him and we are firmly seated *with* Him. Jesus gave us an open portal to see, feel, hear, touch, and taste the many aspects of the glory realm and to be set free from the chains that bind us to this world. I greatly appreciate Dr. Ron Horner's work, study, and life in the heavenly realm. I would encourage all believers to read and ingest the great truths that are manifested in this book *Engaging Heaven for Revelation*.

I add my blessings to you as you gaze into the life above.

Dr. Ron Cohen
Leland, North Carolina

Preface

Over the last several months, Donna Neeper (my Executive Assistant) and I have engaged Heaven on a regular basis as we have sought to understand more and more of the things of Heaven. This book is a compilation of some of the things we have learned thus far. It is labeled Volume 1 because I anticipate successive volumes of a similar nature to follow.

In 1 Corinthians 14:26, the Apostle Paul writes that when believers come together, one would come with a teaching, another a revelation, another a song, and another a tongue or interpretation, so we need to understand that receiving revelation and then imparting it was a common thing in the early church.

Since everyone reading this book grew up in an age in which we are accustomed to the compilation of revelations which forms the Bible, the tendency is to think that new revelation ceased with the passing of the last writer whose material was eventually included in the canonized Bible. However, the personal experience of hearing the voice of the Father, Son, or Holy Spirit speak something to you, or reveal something to you through a dream or vision, still occurs. Revelation has not ceased; we have simply stopped being open to it.

As with all revelation, it will stretch you. If you read this book from your soulish realm and read it as an intellectual endeavor, you will quickly put it down and denounce it. However, if you choose to tell your soul to sit back and call your spirit forward and invite Holy Spirit, who is our teacher and the one who will guide us into all truth, then let Him do the sorting rather than your intellect. Your intellect is typically disqualified from judging spiritual things because it has been trained via the Tree of the Knowledge of Good and Evil, which places the intellect far above the spirit.

We must understand that we are first and foremost a spirit being. We have a soul, and both soul and spirit reside in the earthly suits we call our bodies. The purpose of your soul is to translate to your body what your spirit is perceiving. We are instructed in Colossians 3:1-4 to live from our spirit, as opposed to living from our soulish realm. Allow Holy Spirit to witness to your spirit what is truth.

I know someone who often expresses the idea that if a concept were unknown to them, it therefore could not be true. How they came to this mindset I do not know, nor can I fathom, for many things exist in this earth realm that we do not know about. That does not mean they do not exist. The same is true for the soul realm, and even more so for the realm of the spirit. Just because I have never heard of something before does not mean that it is not true. It may simply have been outside my paradigm to date.

As you read through this book, understand that both Donna and I were stretched on many occasions by what we were learning. However, we are eternally grateful to Heaven for the lessons. The more I learn, the less I really know. Heaven has so much more to teach us.

Contrary to popular belief, we will not be going to Heaven just to be worshipping and playing harps all the time. Heaven is far more than that puny mindset. Will we worship? Yes. Will we be doing it continuously? I doubt it since Heaven is another frame of existence. Heaven is so much more than we have been led to believe. Explore with us these revelations. They may answer some questions for you as well as lead you to a richer understanding of the love of our Father for us and the infinite provision available to us as His children.

In this book, we will share engagements with angels, men and women in white linen, Holy Spirit, and others. Engagements such as these are not uncommon, as they are visible throughout your Bible. However, religion has told us to "be careful," and religion is right. We must be careful of religion that keeps Heaven far, far away, and inaccessible until the end of one's life. We must also be careful of the doctrines of demons that tell us these things have passed away and we should not pursue them. Heaven is as close as your hand and has much to teach us about this earth realm. Let us be ready learners.

It may be necessary for you to take a moment and search your heart for any belief system that causes immediate skepticism to arise within you. Religion has limitations. Some of them are built around the mindset that if organized religion did not teach it to you, then you should automatically reject it. On the other hand, it tells you that you must be careful, or you might get deceived. We can get deceived in our efforts to not be deceived. Some will cite the example of Joseph Smith and how he received a false revelation from the fallen angel Moroni. Joseph Smith and his brother Hiram were active freemasons and had already pledged themselves to be recipients of false light. Joseph Smith was predisposed to deception due to his covenants with freemasonry. If you find these things in your heart, repent before the Lord, and ask the Father to open your heart to what He would have you learn.

Heaven wants to reveal itself to you. May you be able to receive all that Heaven has to show you.

> *I pray that you would be blessed with an understanding heart and a willingness to explore Heaven on your own. May you be blessed with courage and boldness to pursue Heaven whatever the personal costs. May you be blessed with revelation on many levels. May clarity of things long misunderstood be granted to you. May you be willing to engage Heaven in fresh ways.*

Chapter 1
Return to Sender

A few months ago, we sent a small package to a customer, expecting it would be delivered in a matter of days. After nearly four months, we were surprised to see that the package had been returned to us as undeliverable. After checking the postal service website, we saw our address was correct, but they had deemed it undeliverable. It was stamped "Return to Sender." How many times has that happened to us in the realm of the spirit?

Recently, during an engagement with Heaven, we learned that if I chose to bless someone, if I released a blessing to them, and that blessing could not find a landing place in the recipient, then the blessing would return to me, the sender. In that situation, the blessing they would have received is undeliverable because, due to the state of their heart, they were unqualified as a recipient. Wanting to know how that worked, the next day I inquired of Heaven. This chapter summarizes what was learned.

The Scripture that a curse causeless shall not alight contains the same principle (Proverbs 26:2). If no reason exists for a curse to land on someone or something, the curse cannot land. It works that way with curses. If it cannot find a landing place it is "Returned to Sender."

By the same token, if a blessing can be released to someone but is unable to land due to certain sin(s) in that person's life, the blessing returns to the sender, just as a parcel would in our natural world.

Remember that in Luke 6:28, Jesus said to bless those that curse you and pray for them that despitefully use you. To despitefully use someone is to insult, slander, and falsely accuse them. Since the Golden Rule says to do to others as you would have them do unto you, when someone takes it upon themselves to falsely accuse, slander, or insult you, they are stepping in league with the accuser of the brethren. "Your safety in Me," Heaven said, "is that you walk in love one with one another."

When you step into accusation, you have stepped out of love and are leaning toward hatred. Really, you only have two choices: you either love someone or you hate them. If you are actively not loving them, you may be demonstrating hatred toward them. That is not a safe place to be.

John the Apostle understood this. He wrote plainly in 1 John 3:8: He who sins is of the devil. In v. 15 he writes that he who hates his brother is a murderer. If you try to murder someone, either their character or their person, you have stepped out of love and into a place of hatred. Blessing cannot rest on that place.

Therefore, if it cannot land, it must return to the one that sent it. When it returns, it contains the same harvest which was originally sent. If it was a ten-fold harvest when sent, then it will be a ten-fold harvest when it lands upon the sender.

At this point, I still had some questions, but had to take a break from this engagement with Heaven. Shortly afterward, Donna I re-engaged Heaven for more insights.

We asked Heaven for more detail regarding a blessing or curse being released and being returned to you. What we learned from Heaven is as follows:

If it does not have a cause, it does not alight. This is related to the power of the spoken word as referred to in the book of James. Words released are living things. Words released *always* have an effect.

A blessing released is a seed that causes an individual to expand.

A curse that is released is a seed that causes the individual to recede or wither. The result of the curse is the withering of that person. The result of a blessing is the expansion of the recipient.

Think of Jesus and the fig tree. The picture of the withering tree was the result of the cursing. It was a demonstration of the power of God's Word, Jesus, and the swiftness of result—the withering of the fig tree. Notice the swiftness of the result. Curses are designed to bring about a swift result. We can expect the same of a blessing released. A linking exists to the power of life and death is in the tongue that needs to be understood.

A curse that cannot alight comes back on the sender.

A curse is not a language of love. It does not come from the Father's Kingdom but is released out of the dysfunction of the realms of darkness and the darkened areas within an individual, which are those areas of one's life that have not received enlightenment by the Spirit of God. Curses can be released by both saints and sinners, but saints should never be so insensitive as to allow their mouths to release curses. Prophetic intercessors must be exceptionally careful with this.

The Curse

Whether the words released are a curse or a blessing, they must land somewhere. They are a type of impartation, and because the Father's heart is to impart blessing and goodness into the lives of individuals, when you release blessing, it sows itself into a person's realm and has a harvest as the result. This is a principle that God's children are to live by. It is a valuable, beneficial, expansive, glory-initiating, creative act. To release blessing from one's mouth demonstrates the redemption of the tongue through knowing the Savior and the Creator.

This same act, when sowed from a place of darkness, is released as a curse. It is it has a similar effect in the opposite direction. It is not the intention of Heaven and certainly not the desire of the Father that one's mouth would be used in this manner.

Where a curse is released, it is seed sown. If the individual or the individual's realm to whom the curse is released is blessed by God, walks with the Lord in all manner of righteousness, does not have a broken wall of defense, and is enjoined by the help of angels, the curse has nowhere to go and comes back to the one who sent it. The sender reaps their misguided release of power. Words, like deeds, are powerful in their creative role and their effect in the world.

Since the enemy knows this, he uses the wounded and darkened areas of God's people to do his own dirty work to release curses. It does not bother Satan that the individual who releases curses out of immaturity and ignorance would then be harmed by their own release, as his evil contains no balance for that.

However, for a believer to release curses is not the plan of God for that individual. The redemption of that is the awakened realization that they are engaging in self-cursing if they release a curse against someone walking in righteousness. Thus, we have the scriptural principle to bless and curse not. My righteousness protects me, and your righteousness protects you. It provides a deflective shield to cause the curses to return to the sender. It is not the Father's heart that you would release curses in league with the enemy of your soul out of your woundedness and brokenness.

It takes a mindset of the Lord and a oneness with His mind to release a blessing in the face of difficult circumstances. For example, Jesus on the cross, when he requests of the Father that His persecutors would be forgiven for "they know not what they do," is a sincere form of blessing in the face of great obstacles, pain, and hardship.

Since all words are recorded in Heaven, angels pay attention to the saints of God and what is being released from their mouths. Thus, we have the conviction of the Spirit of God within an individual to close their mouth and walk away, as well as the saying in the world, "If you cannot say something nice, do not say anything at all." Would it not be wisdom to withhold one's tongue from releasing a curse out of the hardship of a circumstance?

This is a difficult area for maturing saints, primarily because the soul is in charge of the mouth. In contrast, the believer walking in oneness with God has a sense of Holy Spirit's function to release blessing only and thereby override the soul's tendency to not think in oneness with God.

Quartermaster

Your spirit must act like a quartermaster over your realm to release blessing, not curses. A quartermaster is one who oversees the supplies for a military unit. The quartermaster of your realm, at your request, releases blessing on your behalf.

The supply of blessing increases as you release blessing.

Blessings released in the face of great hardship are noted in Heaven because you, in that instance, have become an overcomer against the plot of the enemy, working from the fallen world in conjunction with the strife of the soul. Your spirit operates like a quartermaster, releasing the blessing of the Father to the members of the Bride, to the Army of God, and to the family of Yahweh.

When the many blessings of God are seen upon the people of God, it defeats darkness, and it causes a friction in those bound in darkness to hunger and desire the blessing of God on His people, on His children, and on His sons.

The abundance of the riches of Heaven come from the release of verbal blessing.

Blessing is Not a Sentiment

Do not be mistaken. The release of the blessings in the name of the King accomplishes much in the body and the Bride of Christ that overflows even to the world. Do not be mistaken that a blessing or the release of blessing by your words is a sentiment. It is not a sentiment. It is not an emotion. It is a spirit-bearing release of the Kingdom's pleasure—the good pleasure of the Father from the Kingdom realm of glory with the intent to increase, expand, and cause growth in the brothers and sisters of Jesus.

Focused Blessing

Heaven says focused blessing is best. Just like the enemy uses a focused curse as a tool of bondage, aim your blessing with more specificity and engage the faith within you as you release it. This is powerful.

A good blessing is the blessing to overcome, stating "I bless you to overcome," followed by the invitation to overcome a specific thing like someone's surgery.

- I bless you to overcome your surgical procedure.
- I bless you to overcome your physical therapy sessions.
- I bless you to overcome pain.
- I bless you to overcome fear.
- I bless you to overcome.

These are true blessings of the Lord. They strengthen and empower another through the expressed hope coupled with firm faith.

It is hope with firmness established in faith.

Another great blessing is the blessing of revelation.

- I bless you for the revealed expression of God in that circumstance.
- I bless you for a revelatory encounter.
- I bless you for a revelation of relationship.
- I bless you for revelation of insight.
- I bless you for revelation of solution.

These are true blessings.

Specific Causes

We asked Heaven, "Are there specific causes for someone to experience the ricochet of a blessing?"

Heaven answered, "All sin should be directed under the blood of Jesus. The sacrifice of the Lamb of God was given that the sin would be made null so that the blessing can fall. This is related to your authoritative release to forgive someone of their sin and bless them, for the Father desires to reach their heart. His redemptive work is at play even now in the hearts of the nations. For example, you might release a blessing to someone, and it returns to you. Instead of that being the end of the story, simply forgive the person for their sin that caused the ricochet effect, bless them again, and release them from the hold the sin had upon them, then re-release the prior blessing to them and they should be able to receive it this time."

The body of Christ is awakening to the adequacy of what Jesus took care of. This is quantitatively being released from Heaven in new ways so that the sons of God awaken to their truest destiny as the releasers of redemption.

Jesus was the gift to take care of the sin problem. All those who come to the Father through Him have forgiveness, but it is the continual work of the spirit to convict a son or daughter of God of their need for forgiveness in areas where they have not walked in perfection. Regardless of what they have done, the blood still speaks forgiveness. This son or daughter, however, must come to receive forgiveness, lest their life be falling away from the living God. It is not that the Father has released him, but that their sin separates them from relationship.

Never do we want to have blessings we have released be returned to sender. We want them to be able to land, but it is good to know that they are never wasted. We will talk about this some more in an upcoming chapter.

May you be blessed with understanding, revelation, insight, and clarity concerning the power of released blessings, in Jesus' name.

Chapter 2
Blessings vs. Bonds

In the prior chapter entitled "Return to Sender," Heaven talked to us about the release of blessings and the landing place for those blessings being receptive. We had further questions, so we engaged Heaven again and continued our instruction on the subject.

We asked Heaven, "Can you comment about the difference between blessing someone and the revelation we have about the Bond Registry and requesting bonds?"

"The Bond Registry is a noted place of Heaven," was Heaven's response. "It denotes enemy activity as well as the legal means to bless and to cause abundant blessing to offset enemy actions of negative, painful, hurtful, and constraining bonds found in that same registry.[1] The Bond Registry revelation offsets what your enemy is

---

[1] A Bond Registry can contain both ungodly and godly bonds. For more understanding see my book, *Releasing Bonds from the Realms of Heaven.*

legally doing because you see it recorded in Heaven, so you come in the same legal manner to offset legal hindrances. The enemy is using ungodly bonds as a legal means against the saints by putting these bonds on the Bond Registry. The negative bond shows up in the Bond Registry against the saint, who then requests both their removal as well as the release and placement of godly bonds on the Bond Registry to offset the ungodly bonds. Thus, the enemy is shut down in using that method because the saints have learned how they can defeat him legally, and he is upset that he has been outdone once again."

The Release of Blessing

The request of the release of a godly bond thwarts the enemy and his demonic hordes from their activity. Isn't it just like the Father to give you two ways to do this, not just one? Do not discount one or the other, for both the release of blessings and the release of godly bonds are incredibly important.

The enemy hopes that by using one, you will not use the other, thereby giving him an inroad in one avenue versus the other. However, when you employ both, you see the double protection, the double abundance, and the double benefit of using both tools.

Bonds have more permanency.
Blessings are more fleeting.

I do not want to impart the impression that blessings are not important, but with the release of a blessing, it is easier for the enemy to swat it down like you would swat down a badminton birdie. It is easier for the enemy to interfere with a spoken blessing than it is with a bond obtained through the Courts of Heaven and placed upon one's Bond Registry. Do not get my meaning wrong here. Both are needful.

The release of blessing is the releasing of the spoken word into the natural realm that affects the supernatural realm. When you use the spoken word to bless, you are receiving from the unseen realm (at least, this is the way it is supposed to work), by the function of the spirit, a release into the natural realm. It combines the spiritual and natural realm, but it comes through your spoken blessing and your sense of what you want to bless them with.

With blessing, you are releasing it to the physical realm with the spoken word from the physical realm. Because it is spoken into the earth realm from the earth realm, it is easier for the enemy to swat it down. For instance, if the blessing cannot land, the enemy has a legal right to swat it down with ease, and it is not able to penetrate or land on the intended subject. In a sense, it bounces back to you because it cannot land. This may be hard to understand, but the enemy has a play in this, a stake in it, or a claim to it, and that is why it cannot land.

Requesting Bonds

Now, contrast that with the request of the release of bonds. This is done by the believer in private, stepping into the realms of Heaven and engaging Heaven to adjudicate his or her own justice from the realms of Heaven. It is released through the authority of the King of the Kingdom realm into the believer's life. Do you see how doing it that way circumvents the enemy in certain ways?

The request for a bond is done from the realm of Heaven within the Courts of Heaven. You are the initiator by requesting the release of the bond from the Court of Titles and Deeds, but it is applied from the realm of Heaven. You are not releasing it into the earth realm. Heaven is releasing it into the earth realm because of its activity and its initiation by you in the realms of Heaven, but it is done in the background. The Bond Registry is the supernatural realm affecting the natural realm.

Can You Circumvent a Blessing that Cannot Land?

We asked, "If I request a bond, does the godly bond released by Heaven to a person's Bond Registry circumvent where a blessing may not be able to land?"

Heaven's answer was, "If you know someone that is in sin, and you still want to see them come into a better place from the work of the Kingdom in the background, you will need to request the release of a bond. The best bond to release is one that is urged by Holy Spirit or a messenger angel. Many times, when in the Court of Titles and Deeds, you can request that the angelic assistants present what Heaven recommends you request. The bond has a better chance of effectual action in the life of the individual than the blessing would because the chance of the blessing not being able to land is higher. Also, you can direct the angels of the other party to be receptive to the work of the Bond Registry angels as they bring the godly bond into that person's realm.

Do you see now that the saints are told to walk in righteousness so that blessings can land? But often, especially with those who are immature in the faith, a bond is the better thing to request because the potential recipient may be in sin or have hidden sin, and the removal of ungodly bonds with the application of godly bonds is a two-fold whammy to offset what the individual is going through.

Do not forget that with the Bond Registry, you are looking at a dual activity, the removal of ungodly bonds and the application of godly bonds. That is a good reminder that it is not just where we appear in court to request the release of ungodly bonds that is important; we also must balance that with the request of godly bonds. That is how Heaven designed these things to work best.

Which to Release?

"How do you know which to release, a bond or a blessing?" we inquired.

"This would depend upon your relationship with the person," was the response. "If you are in proximity with the person and are relatively sure the blessing can land, you will want to bless. If, however, you are dealing with a stranger, such as in Personal Advocacy Sessions, the Bond Registry is the better way to go, remembering again the twofold aspect of the Bond Registry—the removal of the ungodly bonds and the requested release of godly bonds."

Protecting Bonds and Blessings

Next, we queried, "Recently, Heaven discussed with us that during the release of a blessing from Heaven or provision from Heaven and its time of landing in the earth (or manifesting in the earth), in the time in between the release and the landing there exists a vulnerability wherein the provision needs to be protected. If Satan has a claim on a blessing because of the sin in a person's life, is there a way of safeguarding that blessing after it has been released?"

Heaven stated, "This is the activity of the angels. This is the act of the wooing of Holy Spirit to convict that person to operate in righteousness. This is the teaching of the fathers of the faith for the continual relationship with the Godhead—Father, Son, and Holy Spirit—for maturing into all things that are righteous. These are the things that are going to affect what you are asking. The work of the enemy to steal a blessing has always been and will remain his work until his defeat. Saints are called to faith in God, hope, and knowledge of their identity, to come running back to the Father, Son, and Holy Spirit when they have drifted away. This drifting away from relationship the relationship with the Godhead is a lifelong quest to overcome and is sealed by the encounters the individual has with the presence and the glory of God, the miracles, the signs, and the wonders that Heaven is releasing."

Imparting Blessings

"Religion cannot impart blessing. Religious traditions cannot impart blessing. Ritual cannot impart blessing. What imparts blessing is the creative function of the Word. The believer imparts out of the richness of the abundance of God into the realm of that believer that which is hoped for, and that which is seen in Heaven. It is released by one to another from the increasing abundance of the seed that this causes in both realms.

It is huge. It is much bigger than we would know, but we must begin to see it differently and to see it as the sowing of seed."

The sowing of blessing by word is as big as the sowing of tithes, offerings, and alms.

"Imagine if," Heaven stated, "in the face of severe circumstances, a group of believers simply lifted their words in blessing one another; how might things change? The reason you do not see the blessing in its immediacy is because this concept is still in its infancy within the saints. As the saints mature in this understanding, they will see the manifestation of blessings more and more quickly."

"We have experienced some of that when we have the attendees at our meetings pair off and begin to bless one another,"[2] we noted.

Heaven affirmed, "When you have the saints share like that, if they share from the soul realm, it releases in part, but if they share from the position of having their spirit forward,[3] it is like a bomb going off. It is explosive.

"When you do that exercise, you must remind the believer to be in the spirit when releasing blessing to one who is also in the spirit. This is seismic in its impact in the earth realm. What many did in the past was really putting soul to soul, and then they wondered about the

---

[2] Described in *Cooperating with The Glory* by Dr. Ron M. Horner.
[3] See "Learning to Live Spirit First" in the Appendix.

timing, but the soul realm is not the container of the abundance—the spirit realm is.

"Just like with the request of bonds at the unction of Holy Spirit, the spirit-forward man operating in his spirit realm and blessing another individual who is operating from their spiritual realm releasing blessing through the first person to the second by the spoken word is a powerful act. However, if you operate in your spiritual realm from your spirit man and release a blessing but the intended recipient is in their soul realm, they are receiving it in the wrong realm. Therefore, it leads to hope deferred because it is not received in the right realm. If, however, they are spirit-forward when you are sowing a blessing into their spirit, and their spirit realm receives it, it is seismic. The seed of blessing germinates and grows much bigger than what you have yet seen. Receive it by your spirit," Heaven instructed.

A way to maximize this, if you can contact the person (by phone, computer, or in-person), is to say, "I would like to release a blessing to you." If they are receptive, both parties should call their spirit forward, instructing their soul to back up, before releasing the blessing to them. Their part is to receive it, and they can maximize this by speaking from their heart, *"I receive this blessing imparted to me, in Jesus' name."*

Heaven continued, "Remember what I told you about religious traditions. Soul-realm rituals will not be the receptive soil of the word of the blessing that is being released, but you can receive it into your spirit man, or your spiritual realm, by your spirit. A focused, spirit-forward person releasing to a focused, spirit-forward person who actively receives it into their realm produces powerful effects."

In the beginning of this, the soul will need to understand its secondary role in receiving this spiritual blessing of God. The spirit imparts it to the soul, but first, the spirit must receive it. You receive it with your spirit man. When you receive it with your spirit man, you must be "in the spirit" or be spirit-forward, which is also known as being spirit receptive. Your spirit man should resonate with the connection of the other persons' spirit. Here is how you know. When the other spirit-forward individual has successfully received the blessing, the receipt of it should resonate within your spirit realm and you should feel it; you will feel the seed being sown in your spiritual realm. This is all part of being the spiritual people that you are designed to be.

Kingdom Living

Your spirit has an identity of quantitative born-againness[4] as well as a recognition of its position in Heaven and complete acceptance of sonship. Your spirit should operate in these things with increasing revelation, knowledge, understanding, grasp, and stance. Gaining these things, your spiritual stature will

---

[4] Yes, that is how Heaven said it to us.

increase. As it does, your spirit will translate that to your soul.

"Keep moving in Kingdom-living from the Kingdom that is within you," is another way to say spirit-forward. You know how people say, "I receive that?" What if they were saying, *"I welcome that spirit seed of blessing into my spirit realm. I welcome it into my realm, and I assign angels to water that in my realm."* That is like tending the garden of your spirit man with the help of angels who operate in that dimension.

The words of your mouth are typically controlled by your soul, but that is not the way it is meant to be. A redeemed son maturing in sonship should have his words from his spirit. If the whole church, the Bride of Christ, had all their words come from their spirit, it would change a great many things. A confrontation would become an edification because the flow of revelation is in the spirit. This is part of the increasing understanding and maturing of the saints. They are getting stronger in this. *We* are getting stronger in this, but we still have work to do.

The Revelation of Sonship

The revelation of sonship is in direct correlation with the revelation of your identity as a son of God, not a son who does the work of the Father's kingdom, but the son who is loved unconditionally by the Father.

Remember the story of the prodigal son in scripture. We are so much more than we think we are. The Father's good pleasure is to begin to release the Spirit of God to give courage to those willing to risk living from their spirit in this manner. A lot of humanity will miss this. This does not grieve the Father but is not the full measure of His blessing toward humanity through Christ.

Living from the soul alone is not a sin, but neither is it the full plan of God for this generation and future generations. This is what religious tradition, religious teaching, and religiosity through ritual and tradition have tried to squelch, for these are not of the Kingdom of your Father. More and more religious tradition has blinded people from the reality of hell.

Holy Spirit says there is a power surge coming to the earth. There is a power surge coming into the Bride. Not all will choose to walk in the power surge because many will be overwhelmed, just as a power surge short circuits the wiring in many houses. A power surge is coming to the bride to continue the process of her growth and to display the splendors of God to His chosen sons and daughters. As you have received His love and His acceptance through Jesus, the Son, this power surge will sway tall buildings like a jack hammer. It will seem to shake the ground upon which your feet walk. It will bring down ten-story buildings made by man figuratively speaking. It will reduce the rebellious arguments of the world, the arguments of worldliness. It will set aflame a new direction in the church of Jesus

Christ regarding how the church has access to the realms of the kingdom of God and their invitation to that realm.

Chapter 3

Discovering Bridges

One summer day, Donna and I engaged the Help Desk of the Business Complex of Heaven[5] and requested to know what was on our schedule for the day. We were met by Ezekiel (our ministry angel) who wanted to show us the Map Room. Going with him, we entered the Hall of Maps. This place looked like a wing of a building with various rooms along a long marble hall. On the walls one could see various types of maps. Ezekiel explained that these were maps of realms—kingdom realms—including maps for realms that we did not yet know about that contain other beings. "I am not going to tell you a whole lot about these," he said. "What we need is over here."

---

[5] Reference my books, *Building Your Business from Heaven Down* and *Building Your Business from Heaven Down 2.0* for more information.

With that, we arrived at a doorway where Ezekiel simply put his hand up and the door opened automatically. He explained that his angelic DNA and the key that we had given him in an earlier encounter enabled him to open the door in that manner. In this larger room were doorways to smaller rooms. Ezekiel put his hand down on a device and one of the doors of a smaller room opened. In that room were small openings with scrolls in them from floor to ceiling.

Ezekiel informed us that although we saw them as scrolls, they were maps. He took one out, seeming to know which one to go to, and took it to a large table in the outer room. He began to unroll the map to show it to us. As he unrolled the map, his demeanor seemed to change to a very commanding presence as if he were a commander of a military situation.

"You have been talking about your outposts," he explained, "and I want to show you this map of the outposts.[6] So here you are Ron," he said, pointing to North Carolina. Then he said to see it in the form of a bridge. A bridge went from North Carolina (our home base) to Oklahoma (where Donna lives). Another bridge went to our outpost in Nova Scotia, and another to one of our Senior Advocates (also in Nova Scotia). Still another bridge went to Guatemala and another to Belize, where two others of our Senior Advocates live.

---

[6] Outposts are locations where we have a committed presence with representatives who work with our ministry.

He clarified, "These bridges are built through relationship and agreement. One can travel with greater ease on that bridge."

The bridges are built through relationship and agreement. One can travel with a greater ease on that bridge.

"Are you allowed to show us forming bridges?" Donna asked.

"Yes and no," he replied, "Bridges form through agreement with what is written in your scroll."

He showed us a bridge that was in the process of forming with a friend in Atlanta. That bridge looked more like a swing bridge or a rope bridge because it was still forming. The others just mentioned were more significant, like a trestle bridge. On a different engagement with Ezekiel, we had seen a similar thing, but instead of bridges, they appeared as wormholes or tunnels. It was simply a different perspective.

"Remember in the Strategy Room when you saw the sphere, and then you saw the other overlay and you saw the hotspots where the fire was?" (Again, he was referring to an earlier encounter). "That was showing you the warfare against light and dark (not physically the way you saw that, and not that dark has anything over light), but that is where the work of expansion (for the ministry) was and the enemy resists expansion of the Kingdom. This is what we are looking at right now," Ezekiel explained.

Returning to the subject of the bridges and the map, it appeared slightly differently now. Instead of a color, one could little flames like little pieces of the map on fire. We could see one around Kevin in Belize, one around Dianne in Nova Scotia, and a very faint one around our friend in Guatemala. He instructed us to see this from the perspective of what Holy Spirit was warming up. Where you see a greater amount of the burn on the flame, a greater warming up of the hearts of the people by the presence of Holy Spirit and the activity and the work that He is doing is occurring.

"Whose hearts are the warmest? Where is the most work of Holy Spirit in the hearts of men?" Ezekiel asked.

"With Kevin in Belize," we replied, based on what we saw on the map.

"You are perceiving correctly, and Kevin is perceiving as well, and it equates to the call.

"Dianne (in Nova Scotia) is beginning to warm up her group. She is not necessarily saying it in English, but with her own understanding of the advancement and the alignment of the outpost, she is beginning to feel the effect of what this bridge brings her," he explained.

"Can we enhance it, and if so, how?" we asked.

Securing Bridges

Ezekiel explained, "The enhancement comes with the realization that the bridge works two ways. It cannot be all one-sided. Traffic cannot go from you across this bridge all the time without receiving back *from* them at some point.

The bridge is secured
by the two-way traffic.

"You would refer to this as an alliance of agreement where you are sharing resources, praying for one another, and always carrying about in your heart a blessing for one another.

"When the bridge of relationship is not present, or the bridge is broken, it is because something has happened to the two-way traffic. The work of the enemy is to destroy the bridge. If he can destroy the bridge, the network that you are forming is destroyed.

"Lies destroy the bridge. Works of darkness which craft a false story work to destroy the bridge. When a person's heart grows cold toward another person or entity, they stop traveling the bridge and receiving the two-way traffic, and the bridge disintegrates. Some bridges are not meant to be present forever, though. They have timeframes.

"Some people are trying to cross two-way bridges that long ago, they were supposed to cease travelling, but the

Lord has a way of redeeming. When one bridge is destroyed or dismantled, another will usually be built, so it is good to pay attention to the bridges in one's life.

"The bridges that are trying to form are for the purpose of two-way traffic between you and other entities. This is what is going on with you and your Atlanta friend. It is also the way the church aligns, and heart destiny aligns with what is written in Heaven as the perfect will of God, but deeper than that, more dimensional than that, is what aligns according to your scroll," he explained.

Ezekiel continued, "When you are talking to your angels about patrolling your realm, have them patrol your bridges as well." Do you see this as another layer of dimension that angels are given access to when they are given access to the bridges of your life? Commission your angels to patrol the bridges too.

"Let me give you an example," Ezekiel explained, "For instance, you would commission me to patrol the bridges of the ministry. By this command I prevent that which is not supposed to come in from crossing the bridges and I secure the things that are supposed to be coming in on the bridges, including shared revelation, shared blessing, shared resources, shared angelic activity, shared covenants, and more. The bridges of your life need to be secured, as do the bridges of the ministry. Businesses have bridges too that need to be secured.

"These bridges are important for the realms that you are stewarding. That is why you have so many maps, because you have so many different types of entities that the bridges can be built to and secured to, not to mention bridges to other realms and kingdoms based upon divine timing."

When you are talking to your angels
about patrolling your realm,
have them patrol your bridges as well.

With that, the discussion about bridges was over. Ezekiel discussed a few other situations unrelated to the understanding of bridges, but our instruction was clear. We needed to commission him to patrol the bridges to our lives and ministry, which we did.

Take a moment and call your angel(s) nearby. Then, commission them to patrol the bridges of your realms, as well as your realms and gates, and release them to do so. Give them permission to dismantle any bridges that are no longer pertinent to your life so that you only have that which is in your destiny scroll for this time in your life.

Share with us your testimonies of how this has impacted your life.

Chapter 4
The Oil of Courage & Boldness

During another engagement with Heaven, Mitchell, a Man in White Linen who often assists us, started out by asking, "Have you ever wondered where some of this is going?"

Of course, we had wondered, but as Heaven is full of surprises, again we would be quite surprised by what today's revelation brought.

Mitchell began, "A great training is going on in the body of Christ right now which is training feeble spirits. It is training the people of God to become the spirit-filled, actively engaged, spirit-forward men and women of God, so that their last season is less penetrating to their current season. The purpose of this training is so their first response becomes:

> *What is in the realms of Heaven in this moment, in this circumstance, in this situation, in this dilemma, in this problem? What is in the heavenly realm that I can bring into the natural realm*

through the kingdom that flows from within me as I release it to this 3-D world?

Mitchell clarified that this is the training of the saints of Yahweh in spectacular ways.

- Spirits first must be awakened.
- Then they must receive the marriage. I am going to use that term loosely, but there is a type of marrying oneself with the Spirit of the Lord.
- The saints also must learn to make room for Holy Spirit.
- They must learn to receive from Holy Spirit.
- They must learn to hunger after what Holy Spirit can release so that as they mature,
- They must set immature ways of the soul realm aside for the higher realities of the spiritual realm of which they are also a citizen.[7]

"These are coming greater into the body of Christ, but you can know that it will still be a remnant within the body that aligns with this," Mitchell continued.

"Most strongly, this seeking after spiritual realms is a redemption of humanity on a large scale. It is the utter defeat of every lesser kingdom, as Jesus has already won the victory and that victory is now being enforced by the spirits of those raised up in Christ.

---

[7] Colossians 3:1-2

“The manner of spirit walking, spirit-standing, spirit-journeying, spirit-thinking, spirit-syncing with all five spiritual senses have been discussed and disseminated from various outlets in the body of Christ for years.

“We are coming into an engagement with activity now where the saints of God choose by their will to be pursued by Holy Spirit to release the kingdom of God. This will be through the demonstration of their mouth, with their primary agreement being on what Heaven is doing and wants to do in a situation.

“This is to reiterate the importance of recognizing one’s citizenship in heavenly realms, access through Jesus, and receiving of the multitude of gifts consistently being released to those who will receive them by spirit first. After receiving, they must allow their spirit awakening to grow with ever widening understanding. This will raise up a spiritual army who responds instantly to Holy Spirit, together with the angels of the hosts of Heaven, the Counsel Rooms of Heaven, and the cloud of witnesses. This will also lead to growing awareness of their realms and the realms of Heaven as this King of glory begins to make His appearance. Some people will think that the coming of Jesus is tomorrow, which is not what I am saying, continue helping saints to filter their understanding of these new lenses of how spiritual they are. Western Christianity struggles with this the most, but a freeing, an untying, and an unlooping activity of the hosts of Heaven is taking place even now, so that the saints rise up in their spirits with more voracity, more acuity, and more demonstration of this realm of Heaven."

The earth is going to respond to the spirits of man-made one with Holy Spirit.

Mitchell clarified, "These are humans' spirits that will begin to stir and manifest within people as this army of God arises and begins operating. This is the human army of the body of Christ on the earth. There is a need for continued understanding of the supernatural, including the spirit realm, your access in Heaven, and your spirit's receipt (I cannot stress that enough) of spiritual invitations to come up to higher spiritual insights that we must release to you, along with the work of the angelic hosts. This is only going to grow more and more in future days. The supernatural of the realms of Heaven is going to manifest in the natural in the earth realm as it once was."

The deception of humanity has been to only focus on life from the soul realm.

"The soul, having been redeemed, can now rest. The spirit of man now co-laboring, laboring in conjunction with the spiritual realms of Heaven, will manifest the supernatural into the earth realm. And you can count on this. Remember when I first asked you, when I sat down, are you wondering where this is going?" Mitchell reminded us. "This is your answer. All of this is your answer."

Keep Going

Mitchell continued, "Keep going. Keep marching. Deal with the fragments of human souls that come near you for the purpose of their own spiritual unlocking. As that is the work of Holy Spirit in putting them in your sphere, your release of divine understandings and realms of Heaven is the work of unlocking them. Holy Spirit continues with the work of redeeming them.

"A generation behind us is coming that is going to move in greater signs and wonders. They are being warmed up, having been awakened and having been hidden for a time.

"Begin to ask the Father for these to come near the language that you are releasing. Many will not have been bound by previous seasons of religious thinking. And they may come to you because their spirit is awakened, but it is still young. Many saints who are beginning to be awakened in their spiritual understandings are coming to new depths of understanding about how controlled and manipulated they have been, and how they have operated in conjunction with evil spirits for the purpose of the spirits of control and manipulation. It is beginning to crack off them like a hardened shell that has settled on them without their knowledge. As they free themselves from the limitations of the need of their soul to manipulate or control, new freedoms in the Body of Christ will be released. These new freedoms require one thing and that is trust—the free fall trust that God will catch you, that Yahweh is on His throne, and that he has His ways.

"The supernatural cannot begin to manifest if the spirits of control and manipulation are also manifesting. Evil spirits of control and manipulation will seek to steal the result of the supernatural. I urge you not to align with the evil spirits of manipulation and control. Allow the purging of your family bloodlines regarding these two things. Many are walking through these things now, and it is for this purpose—so the supernatural can manifest that one is set free from the hidden agenda of spirits of control and manipulation.

"We need the reverent fear of the Lord. That is the opposite spirit, to let the Lord be God. It is surrender to Heaven and its manner of operation to allow God and Holy Spirit to be who they are and do what they want to do."

Mitchell went on, "Remember Philip, the evangelist who obeyed the promptings of Holy Spirt and went to the Ethiopian eunuch and taught him from the scriptures? That is an example of someone who was surrendered to obedience to the Father. That is coming back in this day and it is the result of a function of Holy Spirit in man."

Chapter 5
The Spirit of Counsel

We had been engaged with Heaven and were receiving revelation when Donna became aware of another being with us. It did not seem to be a Man in White, nor an angel. We did not have a grid for this encounter. Counsel (as in the Spirit of Counsel) had appeared. Quickly, we stated, "I receive counsel. I invite counsel to release the Word of the Lord."

He appeared in the form of a lampstand. We invited Counsel to help us understand, and he began to explain that Counsel is released to the people of Yahweh as they honor and make room for Counsel. Counsel is a lampstand. He is a light, and he illuminates what we call the avenue or the function of becoming enlightened—not from anything outside Yahweh, but only within Yahweh. He is Yahweh's counsel. A deep reverence and a holiness could be sensed. He continued, "Basically, this message is to ask the Lord Yahweh to walk among the Counsel of His Counsel. Do not harden your heart to counsel or counsel's input. Soften your heart to the Counsel of Yahweh. The People of God are going to need counsel."

Our response was to say, "I just say to you, Counsel, you are welcome to walk in my realms. I welcome you in my gate. Teach me to honor you and respect you. Show me where I have neglected to do that and help me to understand how to walk with you. Come walk with me and change me. Come walk with us and change us. Come walk with the people of God and change us."

Counsel said, "You are having trouble perceiving me because you're looking with only one set of eyes. Keep looking, keep looking."

Suddenly Donna exclaimed, "You are Isaiah 11:2, the Spirit of Counsel." Having said that, she could feel the Sevenfold Spirit of God in undulations as they revealed themselves, but they were all revealing themselves around and with the primary reflection of the Spirit of Counsel.

Counsel continued, "This is my message to God's people. Invite me in their realms. I want to walk with them. I want them to know me. I want them to know when I have spoken and when they have heard me. I want them to know when they have responded correctly to me and this begins with honor and respect. This respect is different from human respect. This is reverential. It is knowing you are able to have relationship with the Spirit of Counsel, but it is different."

We chose to receive what Counsel brought and deposited. We invited Counsel into all our realms and into every territory of our realms. We chose to agree with moving in tandem with Counsel, walking with Counsel, hearing from Counsel, meditating on Counsel, allowing Counsel to give us courage, allowing Counsel to give us boldness, and allowing counsel to show us the way we have not been before. We were ready to walk as children.

Donna suddenly noticed two scribing angels with us. We asked, "What are you writing down?" We discovered that they are assigned to Counsel and they always make record of his appearing.

"I recognize and them and I am in agreement with the full receiving of Counsel," Donna replied for both of us.

The Oil of Courage

A Man in White Linen then appeared.

"Hello, what do you have for us?" Donna asked.

She then saw a box. She removed the lid and the box inside was full of oil. We learned it was for distributing to the people on our weekly mentoring group. We were instructed, "Release it to the people, distribute it. Have angels come and distribute it to them. Have angels come in and mark their foreheads with this oil.

"Have them verbally state that they agree if their heart agrees to receive this anointing. Have them check their hearts first. If they have doubt in their hearts about receiving this oil, they are not to receive it, but to wait until their hearts are free of doubt." The man plainly said, "Heaven is not interested in wasting this oil on those who have doubt. This is for the saints of God who are seeking belief with all their hearts. It's for courage to know Him who backs you up."

"Do you see why this must be received without doubt?" the man asked.

He continued, "This is not a time for doubt. This is a time for belief and courage to believe what Yahweh has said and what He has spoken."

He anointed Donna's forehead with the oil, and she described it. "Wow. I can really feel that. This stuff is amazing. It gives you such strong belief. It leaves no room, no cracks for doubt to get in. It makes you courageous."

Donna began to declare, "Oh, I receive courage in my spirit. I receive courage in my soul. I receive courage in my body. I receive courage at my gate, and I agree for courage to manifest through my vessel, and word, and deed, and attitude. I agree to be aligned with courage. I agree to work with courage, too. I agree to work in tandem together with courage." She was suddenly aware of a boldness that was hard to describe.

"This oil is twofold," he said. "Describe it like this: you know how when you eat something that is both salty *and* sweet, you get one and then you get the other? The boldness comes on the end of the courage. The courage was first and now it is a boldness. It is a release of boldness."

Donna continued, "It is like I didn't taste the boldness until I tasted the courage, but now I taste both."

The Man in White said, "This oil purifies the sons of Levi." He said, "You are not going to have very much understanding about this because it is layered and deep, but the purification of the sons of Yahweh by this is happening now within the body of Christ and among the saints. It is a sort of purifying. It has a future use. It has a future display as a future manifestation."

Donna could discern a change within her spirit. "It has changed in my spirit," she explained.

The man kept saying the same thing. "Courage and boldness without doubt. Courage and boldness without doubt for the manifestation of faith—for the utilization and the release of faith."

Take a moment right now and invite the angels to minister this Oil of Courage and Boldness. Search your heart for any doubt and repent for any doubt. Determine that you want the Father most of all and invite the angels to anoint you with Courage and Boldness for the days ahead.

Chapter 6
Plundering the Enemy's Camp

Provision is being released, but the provision trains[8] need protection. This provision is from the Father's storehouses. The delivery of provision also has a timing component to it, so as a release of the provision, it needs to be protected as well.

> *We do charge and commission our angel(s) and their ranks to protect the provision that is coming to us. Protect it on its way. See that what has been slated for release comes to manifestation.*

"Are there weapons that you need for that?" we asked.

In our situation, we knew he had maps, but he requested something called guideposts. These are recognized by angels. On earth we have traffic signals on thoroughfares. Angels have guideposts and know the

---

[8] The trains that carry the provision.

markings of the guideposts. We made the request of the Father and Heaven continued in our instruction.

Heaven told us that we need to begin to think in terms of offense, not defense, regarding the provision that the Father has for us. Ezekiel was suggesting an offensive stance. He explained, "There is provision that comes based on your giving, your offerings, and your obedience where you see the field that is yours—the ministry's field—where you know you have harvest. It is good to make sure it is protected."

Defense would be where we go to the Court of Reclamation and get back what the enemy stole, but offensive measures are about the provision *that is being released.* This comes from the faith that you have that you know you will be receiving the provision and you are expecting it. You have done things such as make withdrawals from the Finance Department for it, sown in obedience, and so on. It is an offensive stance of protection over the coming prosperity, the release of windfalls, and things like that. We need to learn how to protect it offensively.

Rain from Heaven

Lydia, a Woman in White Linen who serves as our business advisor,[9] came to assist us. We asked her to help us understand.

She began, "It is not as hard as you think. Think of provision as rain from Heaven. The rain is coming, and you must put out your pots to receive it. The time between when it leaves the clouds and when it ends up in the pot is what needs protecting."

Therefore, we need to charge our angel(s) and their ranks to offensively and aggressively war against the theft or potential theft, derailment, or capture by rerouting of the rain of the provision that has been released from the Father to the ministry. This would involve commissioning our angels to do this. Ezekiel has maps that he uses for this as he instructs his ranks to an offensive position, not just defensive.

It is the difference between telling the ranks of angels to protect, but you can also instruct them to plunder.

The heavenly host is not looking for a fight from the enemy because they know whose they are and they

[9] This is explained and demonstrated in my books, *Building Your Business from Heaven Down* and *Building Your Business from Heaven Down 2.0.*

know the fight is already won, but when the fight comes to them and the enemy makes an attack, you have traditionally stationed your angels to defend what is yours, but...

Now release them also to not only defend what is yours, but to plunder the enemy's camp.

Wouldn't you want that? To plunder is to make Satan pay when he brings the fight, and he loses.

Always make him pay by plundering the enemy's camp.

Lydia instructed, "Do not think of camp as singular. Rather, think of the many camps of the enemy from which he attacks you, the staff, the clients, the communication lines, and the provision. Release your angels to war *defensively*, but ***also** offensively* to plunder the enemy's camp and gain back what belongs to the Kingdom of God. This would be a warfare activity that Ezekiel is well equipped for." At that point, Ezekiel was demonstrating his agreement with this and his 'can't wait' attitude.

Now Lydia showed a sack of gold and said, "All the gold and all the silver is the Father's.[10] The enemy has for

---

[10] Haggai 2:8

eons collected the gold through various means and by various ways, but now is the time to release your angels to plunder the enemy's camps and get back the gold."

"Do you see there is a difference here in the reclamation court where you go for legal means?" Lydia asked. "You can also release angelic activity to plunder the enemy's camp. Therefore, where the enemy has stolen from people who do not even know how to get back it back,

---

Heaven is saying the gold can be retrieved by any who will.

"To get the portion of it back is the Father's goal, but if you are the one who gets it back, it is credited to your action (the one who is releasing the angels to the task) in some measure, **no matter who forfeited it.** It is still God's gold. Someone just must retrieve it. This falls to the mature saints of God who understand the ways of Yahweh and who are already operating in obedience as true sons," Lydia stated.

We asked to be coached in this process and we were told, "It is like a commissioning in which we charge Ezekiel and his ranks so we can capture from the enemy that which has been stolen. Heaven wants to restore to us things that have been stolen, not only from us, but from those that we minister to or from those are associated with the ministry and their families, from their future, or from their past. In every arena, we are plundering to recover all that has been stolen, in Jesus' name," Lydia explained.

"When the angels recover the bounty, what is the distribution of that?" we asked.

Lydia answered, "It comes back to the one who requests it. See your angels as mighty warriors.

Your angels can get what is yours, but they can also get whatever is available.

If you plunder an enemy camp and you see an object that he took from someone you know, you can say, 'I am going to go get that. I see where the enemy took this whole room full of treasure from the kingdom of God, so I claim that too.' That is the plundering of the enemy's camp."

We do not really need to understand or see the distribution. We will just experience it. We will just do this and see what happens.

How to Speak to Your Angel(s):

"We commission you to go to your defensive stance in protection of the provision coming to us.

We also commission you to your offensive stance for you and your ranks.

We commission you to offensively plunder the enemy's camp, gain what has been stolen and return it to where it needs to go, in Jesus' name."

If you are a Kingdom citizen and the Kingdom has been plundered, you are loosing angelic hosts to get back whatever the Kingdom lost, whether it is yours or not. This is your right. You have a right to that, but you are also operating as an ambassador of the Kingdom to get back what belongs to the Kingdom and let the King determine what he will do with it. Heaven just wants it back, but Heaven needs sons who will stand in their place as sons and see to it that the plundering of the enemy's camp occurs. Saints take your place!

Chapter 7
Coming Changes

This chapter is a directive from Mary, a Woman in White Linen, who serves as one of our business advisors.[11]

Mary began, "A change of season is fast approaching, A new revelatory flow is going to appear, and I am letting you know so you will be aware of the change. Nevertheless, continue what you are doing, stepping into, and expanding in it.

"You are forming a creation with the Father to expand people's understanding, and to give them a surfboard to surf on because of the wave of God that is coming into the earth for the people of God, for those whom He has called. It will be a new wave of the membership of the body, a wave of divine remembering of who the Bride really is and what she is here to do. It is

[11] Lydia serves as our chief business advisor but has others who serve with her.

also a new wave of coping with what the enemy stirs up and even releases from Counsels of Darkness that are already overcome by the overcomers in Jesus."

Mary continued, "You have been building surfboards for individuals to plant their feet firmly upon, to ride the cascading waves of new revelation coming into the earth regarding a great variety of things. As you press in, this will feel like a diminishing of thinking and a heightened concern with operating *in* the Spirit *from* the spirit with more ease. It will be allowing the guidance of Holy Spirit, which is the wave under the surfboard, to continue forward with the plans of the Father."

Further explaining, Mary said, "Some have been swimming in this wave, but they need a surfboard to engage with it in a more directed fashion. Just like a surfer engages the wave upon which he rides with the steering of the surfboard, what you are giving people is a way to help them steer through what is presently about them and what is coming. It will help them ride the wave for the greatest gain, not only in their lives, but in their Kingdom lives and in their fresh realization of their authority in Jesus, His Kingship, and His authority that is in the believer's life.

"A new birthing is coming of a great many things. This is a positive word I am giving you and one you can distribute, because what the people need today is hope for the future, lest they fall in pits of hope deferred and despair. Remind them again to speak in tongues. Remind them again to give freely and seek the kingdom of God. A refreshing is on the way."

She expounded, "By October you will be ankle deep in the refreshing. This is a spiritual refreshing I am speaking of. The refreshing comes first to the spirit and the spirit man, and then manifests however slowly to the physical realm, but all things are timely and being timed. Keep going forward.

"There is still a plan of fear to the disrupt people of God as they gain this momentum. Fear will be used again, and the people have got to get up and get set free from fear. Do not align with fear no matter what your natural eye sees. A way out exists for the people of God—it always has," Mary said.

Infusing Courage and Boldness

She went on, "Continue to draw on the infusion of courage and boldness you received in recent days. Continue to request that it be poured out, continue to release it to others, and continue to let it stir within your being. Continue to allow this anointing of courage and boldness to change how you speak and the way you view what is in your natural circumstance. The people of God are going to be noted for courage and boldness. It is time for courage and boldness, for how do you cross over into the promises unless you have courage and boldness?

"Practicing courage and boldness as well as riding the current wave will help you wade through the waters of disruption in coming days more quickly. This will be because you have become practiced in courage and boldness and have increased your understanding of where it comes from and how to utilize it by obtaining it from the Father. Courage and boldness are leadership qualities, and right now the world needs the leadership qualities of the Bride in this.

"Ask the Father for the language of courage and boldness. Ask the Lord for the words of courage and boldness so that you are writing courageously and boldly; so that you are speaking courageously and boldly; so that your ear is hearkened to those who are speaking also in courage and boldness. Courage and boldness are qualities that will be followed in days ahead.

"Those who speak without courage and boldness will evidence a lack of forward movement and a trust in God to achieve and attain the goal of forward movement.

Deal with Your Bond Registries

Mary instructed, "Check the bond registries of the people you know and share your findings with your audience. Create a revisitation of the bond registry to remove the influx of ungodly bonds even now being placed by the enemy to cause men's hearts to fail."

Continuing, she said, "When a population begins to feel like they are finally moving forward and they begin to think, 'Oh, things are getting back to normal,' they sometimes experience another let down. Right when they are beginning to have hope, another let down comes. This is worse than the first let down because it causes men's hearts to fail. It causes mankind to lose hope.

"Visit the bond registries of the people around you," she instructed, "and start talking about this with your group so that you are pressing in. Remove in advance the ungodly bonds of hopelessness, hope deferred, woundedness from hopelessness, and all things related. You cannot enter the next season if these are at work. Then fill the bond registry with the hope of God, the hope of endurance, the hope of glory, the hope of manifested faith made visible, the hope of breakthrough, the hope of achievement, and the hope of overcoming.

"It is the hope of these things that causes you to receive and gain the things for which you are hoping. In future days, your audience will need to have a revisitation of hope. Strong hope carries a people forward. Strong hope needs to be written on the soles of your shoes. Strong hope needs to be written on the thongs of your sandals. This strong hope needs to be the path upon which you walk, and for this, courage and boldness must be received in advance so that you walk in a hopeful manner.

"Many do not understand, when the heart carries hope and faith, how pleasing this is to the Father. There is an element of hope for a good, expected outcome that will increase and enlarge the people of God in days ahead. I am talking about those who seek God, those who are hungry for God, but have not found Him, and those who are being rescued so that they may have hope. I am announcing today, in this round table discussion regarding LifeSpring International Ministries, the release of hope.

"You can talk to your weekly people (CourtsNet) about this, your Tuesday people (the Courts of Heaven Mentoring Group) about this, and your blog audience about this—the need for courage and boldness, so that hope can be tied on like shoes and they can walk in them on the path of hope. There is grace for this hope, and this is one aspect of the wave. There is a grace for hope coming to those who will receive it.

"While the enemy plans a dart like a fiery arrow into the heart of mankind to lose their hope once again, the people of God, those who have ears to hear, will have understanding in advance of that dart. You are going to receive the courage and the boldness to tie on your shoes of hope so that you can keep moving forward. Therefore, the dart is not going to find its mark," Mary explained.

Everyone around the table was leaning in on every word being spoken. With LifeSpring, there is a commonality of thought that says, "We are just going to keep going." To reiterate this, George,[12] William,[13] and Mary stated together, "We are going to keep going."

---

[12] George is our advisor in the Finance Department.

[13] William is of our business advisors along with Lydia and Mary.

"Everything that you are doing with live stream, you are just going to keep going. It is going to keep going," Mary finished.

Permission to Hope Again

At this point, William said, "Give permission to people to hope again. Give those who have sight of the ministry's social media and all the things where people see what we are putting out. Let the people's sight be focused on hope. Do not forget, you must tie courage and boldness to it. It will take both in this era or season to move forward. Even now other leaders who are beginning to show forth the same message of hope."

He continued, "For the people of God it is a warfare tactic of hopeful expectation of victory and of gaining the goal for which you went to war. It is a thing. It is a substance. I know we say that about faith, but this is what hope is like."

Request Vessels of Oil

William reminded us, "Ask the Father for continued vessels of oil for courage and boldness. Request this for your listeners, those who see and hear you, that they be given vessels of oil as well. These are vessels of oil for hope. This oil enables or eases one to receive hope. Envision giant barrels of oil. Request this oil."

He asked for us, "Why is it these barrels of oil ease the way for hope?"

"If you have need of this, you must buy[14] this from the Lord,"[15] we were told.

Lydia, who had joined the meeting began, "Individuals access the vessels of oil by requesting the oil that is being poured out and made available from Heaven. Request angels to bring the oil to those around you."

Fill Your Eyes with Hope

Lydia continued, "Be careful what your physical eye is filled with because if you are concentrating on darkness and its deception, that is what you are going to get your eye full of. You need to fill your eye with the Oil of Hope.

"If something does not agree with or release hope, is there any reason to fill your eye with it?

"Be careful in days ahead of what you are filling your eyes with. The enemy works to fill our heart with fear through the eye gate and the ear gate, so you must fill your ear and eye gate with this Oil of Hope.

---

[14] Request it of the Father.
[15] This felt like the oil that the wise virgins had in Matthew 25.

"Remember, oil is slippery. When you fill your eye gate and your ear gate with the Oil of Hope, the enemy slips, and slides. He cannot get traction when he tries to come in through the same gate.

"Ask the angels of God to fill your eye gates and your ear gates with the oil that enables hope. Give yourself permission to question everything that does not contain hope. The promises of God which are hope-based are the promises of God to hide in your heart. By all this counsel, you are being prepared to circumvent plots of the enemy," Lydia concluded.

Chapter 8
Communication Pathways

Ezekiel began one encounter by asking, "Remember yesterday's lesson when I showed you how you can meet with me in the realms of Heaven versus when I step into your atmosphere at a different frequency and you are aware of it?"[16]

"Yes, I remember that lesson," Donna replied.

As Ezekiel spoke about that encounter, which was also a lesson, the same effect was noted again. It was so subtle that Donna almost missed it. First, Ezekiel was distinguishable in the earth realm in Donna's office, but then with virtually no distinction, she was with him in the realms of Heaven. She did not even realize that she had stepped in.

"Angels can step in to get your attention. Spiritual beings will step in to get your attention. You had an

---

[16] This chapter is also in *Engaging Angels* by Dr. Ron M. Horner.

experience with Counsel and then with a Man in White Linen with a box of oil. And you had experience with me stepping near you and your own angels," remarked Ezekiel.

Let me give you some backstory Donna explained to me. "I'm reading a book titled *Systematic Theology for the New Apostolic Reformation*, written by Dr. Harold R. Eberle. It was a gift from a friend back in February. I got busy with LifeSpring and just let it go by the wayside until one Saturday, I felt like I heard the Lord saying, 'Go pick up that book! Do not start with the Foreword, start with chapter one, and just work your way through that book,' so I did.

"This morning, I had just finished with the chapter where the author is talking about time where he is talking about how time is relative and what science says about the relativity of time and how this fits in theology. When you begin to pursue what and how you think about time and why you think about time like that, it is quite enlightening. His basic point in the entire book is that most of Western Christianity has a Plato foundation, and this is where classical and reformed theology comes from. Dr. Eberle was just noting some differences and some points about how he thought this way at one point too, but now he does not think that, and he explains why. He calls it the Father-Son Theology. I am reading the chapter on time and I am fascinated because I am interested in that kind of thing. Dr. Eberle has this description of how to understand what his point is, and he says most of Christianity thinks 'God is outside of time,' but what they really mean is 'God is eternal.' What this leads to as a conclusion is that God is not in the present with you—like you are in the present and that the future is coming towards you, but the future is not known yet. And he said that this comes from thinking God is outside of His creation, not inside His creation.

"I understood that," she stated. "He says if you begin to think of time coming toward you and time is passing you, but you are in your present, the future is never settled for a lot of reasons because it is still not known, as it is coming towards you. He says you can have some thoughts about how it could be and should be." I am sure he is going to unpack this more, but this is Donna's quick grasp. You are getting the bullet points.

She resumed, "I began to realize, 'He is pointing out some things in my belief system that made me think, wow, that's going to need a good tweaking, because I don't think I could go forward thinking about that the same way.' But if you think of it in the way he explained, then everything that you and I are doing with Courts of Heaven and stepping in the realms of Heaven works better.

"This morning after I finished reading that, I stepped out onto the back porch and I was just standing there. I said to the Lord, 'Well, there is something about this time thing that is important that you are really trying to show me. And I am just going to say, I surrender to know what it is. You are trying to help me understand because I think it is tied to the phrase, 'The Kingdom of God is within You.'"

Donna continued, "Let me go back to just a few seconds ago, when all of a sudden I felt the presence of time and I said, 'I don't know what that is,' and Ezekiel said, 'That's time.'"

Ezekiel said, "Remember, I wanted to come to this conference room to continue talking about what was discussed yesterday, how you can perceive me here in your room. It is as if I am standing there, then you see me with spiritual sight, or you perceive me with spiritual knowing. When I come like that in my presence, your body is aware of it, meaning it has manifested so that your spirit knows as soon as you open eyes and ears to see me. Your soul is the last to know, but it eventually gets the memo.

"Just now you had the experience where I was right there, and then without any perceptible change, you and I were here," Ezekiel continued. "I am talking to you about time because it is all the same. It is the present moment. You were not asking this question, but I am showing you that there is an element of time affected by spiritual realms.

Timing dimensions are affected by the result of spiritual interactions.

You can define this by your knowing or perception of angelic beings who want to be in the present with the sons of God. They want the interaction. Both angels want and men and women in white linen want this.

Ezekiel noted, "It is not that they want it. It is that this is the way it can be. This is the opportunity. This is the richness of the kingdom in which you dwell."

He continued, "Many people are thinking that angelic beings are coming from a different time dimension and they are stepping into your time dimension. We are all in the present together. It is a relational dimension of time we both exist in." Ezekiel ended this segment by saying, "I'm going to let you chew on that for a while."

Communication Pathways

Ezekiel went on to explain, "Communication pathways exist between angels on assignment and those who are living on the earth. I am going to share some deep things with you about the angelic realm—the hosts of Heaven. Remember in scripture where it is written that Jesus knew the thoughts and intent of men's hearts? He did that several times.[17] When they were going to throw him off the cliff,[18] Jesus knew. That is one example. Remember when he is talking to the Pharisees and he knows the thoughts and intents of their hearts."[19]

---

[17] Matt 9:4, 12:25, 15:19, Luke 5:22, 6:8, 11:17
[18] Luke 4:29
[19] Matt 12:25

Ezekiel explained, "Jesus knew this because an angel related it to Him. Although humans have always assumed this was Holy Spirit speaking, at that point in time, Holy Spirit had not been given as resident within believers on the earth. Holy Spirit was still in Heaven, not on the earth. When Jesus engaged with the Father, he would 'go up to the mountain,'[20] which is code for 'step into Heaven.' The angels knew and translated it to Jesus in His natural body. Remember, Jesus set aside His glory and operated as a man while on earth. How did Jesus know that? It was translated by angels to Him. This is the work of the angelic. They do this only for purposes of the expansion of the Kingdom of God and from what is being written and spoken of the Father. The knowledge that angels have is highly valuable to satanic occult forces and is often why angels are captured by realms of darkness."

Ezekiel continued, "The angels that are now the hosts of Heaven are extremely loyal. They do not divulge information to the wrong people who are operating with the wrong assignment or with the wrong realms or kingdoms and beings of darkness.

Angels are meant and designed to operate with the believing saints.

"Notice I said the believing saints. The believing saints who believe that angels can and do bring messages

---

[20] Matthew 17:1, Mark 6:46, 9:2, Luke 9:28

to them from the Father's Kingdom can interact with the angelic realm to receive these messages. That is why they are called messengers.

A message is simply
a communication.
It is a sharing of information.

"**The beings of Heaven can translate this to the spirits of humans who are sanctified and being continually redeemed by their seeking after Jesus and the Kingdom of God**. The messages that they bring are going to be especially important to pay attention to in the coming days. This communication pathway is greatly contended over by forces of darkness who seek to spy, to hear, or learn so that they can put together, like a jigsaw puzzle, the plan of Yahweh to bless the saints with His power and might, His goodness and kindness, and His plan to redeem humanity.

"In the dark realms, spying is ancient practice. They have done this a long, long time and are very adept at it. However, greater understanding and receipt of messages from the angelic hosts is coming to the Body of Christ, the Bride, so that she can operate in tandem with the Bridegroom.

"While the Bridegroom is not what you would call physically present in the earth realm now, He is present with her in the spiritual places where He has given access for the saints to join Him and to conduct business on His behalf.

"The basic nugget you need to know is that angels are messengers, and they are being released more and more frequently now from Heaven and they have many things to share. They are coming to earth frequently now.

The messages of angels come for the present.

"They are not necessarily revealing the future, because as you are learning, *the future is forming*. The Father is counting on His sons and daughters to form the future with Him.

"One day you might be doing something as simple as brushing your teeth and suddenly you have a knowing or you see a connection about something. Suddenly, a dot connected to something you needed insight on, and the information is dropped into your spirit. That was an angel bringing a message to you," Ezekiel explained. "You are learning and are being trained not to discount the messages you have been receiving from angels.

"Some in the body of Christ have been taught (especially in prophetic streams or in charismatic arenas) that the only one speaking to you (or allowed to speak to you) is Holy Spirit; that He is the only one bringing you these messages. Heaven acknowledges that you respect Holy Spirit, but Holy Spirit's work is also working with angels. Holy Spirit and angels are working together, and messages are being delivered into the earth with more frequency and with greater ability. Angels now have more ability to deliver these messages with greater constancy and frequency. It seems only a small remnant of the body of Christ is receiving angelic messages, but this is global; it is not in the United States alone.

"For a long season, messages were brought in the form of dreams, but in more recent times, the messages are coming directly to our spirits as our spirits are gaining freedom and liberty to receive. That is why the teaching of the realms of Heaven and the teaching of the Courts of Heaven and the teaching of spiritual senses involving the imagination is giving new language for people to understand the true purpose of their sanctified imagination. All these things are useful in what we call the communication pathway between humans and angelic beings.

"The church has been caught in a loop where they were looking in the wrong direction for many years," Ezekiel explained. "They were looking at demons and the activity of demons when all they had to do is turn their head to see the activity of the angelic hosts. Angels are more numerous and are greater in power in every respect.

Wrong Alignments

"Some humans in the earth have chosen realms of darkness and aligned themselves with lesser kingdoms to accomplish for the temporal moment what we refer to as power. Little do they know that what they surmise to be an increase in their power is sealing their eternity. In the world you are going to be aware of the activity that these people have aligned with and stirred up. Their activity opens portals that allow in dark spirits to afflict others.

"I want to give you a real, kindergarten understanding of this occult activity, of rituals, sorcery, and what witchcraft stirs up. Occult activity opens portals for dark spirits to come in. When those dark spirits come in, those who come in league with them do the dirty work of the demonic entity. This is what has happened over Portland, Oregon in 2020. A dark portal was opened that the angelic forces are working to close. A flood of demon spirits and other dark beings have come through that portal. The result of what has happened is clearly seen in humanity being afflicted by the dark spirits. You can know that this was done intentionally and has been done in other places of the globe as well, with equal intention.

"Know that it has not gone unnoticed by Heaven, by the Counsels of Heaven, by the angelic realm, and by the forces of Yahweh who will shortly put this down," Ezekiel clarified. "Coronavirus and its manipulation about the earth was a similar activity by the forces of darkness. Let me give you a caution: this information is not for babies; it is meat, not milk.

"Let us get back to the basics—that the angels of Yahweh have been released in greater numbers and with more frequency to bring the messages to His people for many reasons, such as protection or to open new areas of understanding that humans are going to walk in. Some angels are bringing revelation of how man can help man, displaying the goodness of God on the earth," he added.

Knowing When Your Angel is Speaking

I (Ron) have been instructed to walk lightly in this area of releasing this information because it is going to be self-evident in the days to come. I have been suggesting to you that you can have conversations with angels, but you may not have understood that your angels are having conversations with you. That is the point that I want to illuminate—how to know when your angel is speaking to you.

It is going to come through your human spirit from the perception of your spiritual senses. Yes, your spiritual senses must be trained, disciplined, cleansed, and focused with the intent and desire of use that is sometimes resisted. It is resisted from the soul realm of a person *and* from outside dark activity *and* from doctrines of demons *and* from minds which have not fully aligned with the mind of the Lord Jesus Christ.

Let me go back to something I said before. Remember I said this all has a purpose, and its purpose is for the expansion of the glory of the Kingdom in the earth realm. It is also expanding the territory of the Kingdom within people. Do not let this shock you, but it is expanding the Kingdom realm in heavenly places as well.

I remind you again, what you hear from Heaven is often quite a hefty serving. It is not for the babies. Courage and boldness are given to the body of Christ to eat this full meal, engage, and receive the expansion that courage and boldness gives you. Courage and boldness have an activity that have not been fully understood. The Oil of Courage and Boldness is from Heaven. It is Heaven's courage and boldness. It is not the soul realm's courage and boldness, and it has its own effect.

Some people heard what I said recently about courage and boldness, and they stirred up their souls in courage and boldness. While this is not bad, it can be used for evil and that will wound people. When you use courage and boldness from your spirit man in conjunction with Holy Spirit, it has a completely different effect, expanding the kingdom of God. That is a weighty matter, but it is at work on your behalf.

Chapter 9
The Coming Increase in the Release of the Glory

This particular Friday morning started out as usual. Around mid-morning, Donna and I accessed Heaven's Help Desk and were instructed that we had a meeting scheduled. A gentleman came forth (a Man in White Linen), and after a moment, Donna recognized him as Joseph of Arimathea. She had encountered him several months prior, and he had come to speak to us about a coming release of The Glory. We were taken to a conference room near some classrooms in the Halls of Heaven. It was different from where we usually met someone. The conference room resembled a small sitting area with some chairs around a coffee table, like a conversation pit.

He started by saying, "It's time for the exposure of the doctrines of demons. These doctrines," he said, "have come up against a timing of Yahweh. Light exposes all darkness. Light encroaches where it is not welcomed by darkness, and darkness cannot hide."

"Do you understand what I mean?" he asked. "When I say that the power of light against darkness is total, it is overwhelmingly complete. It would be good for the saints to understand that where they operate in the light, they so completely overwhelm darkness that it is impossible—yes, I am using that word, impossible—for darkness to remain anywhere near the release of light from their inner being—their spirit man. This understanding is going to be necessary in coming days. I want to teach you so that you can teach others how to release the light." Thus, we began our instruction.

Joseph began, "First, here are a few basic things to understand. Light is made of wavelength frequencies and your physical body is created to not only hold it, but to release it. You have experienced this before in what you call the glory realm. When you are near the presence (the glory), it touches the physical body, and the physical body manifests it. What is manifesting is the wavelength frequency of that glory.

"The light of glory emanates from the Father's throne—from the mercy seat—from absolute glory."

"Now, when you say that phrase, 'absolute glory,' that takes on a different connotation to my understanding. I don't have a definition for it, but I get what you're saying," Donna remarked.

"Power magnified beyond your understanding is absolute glory," Joseph declared.

He continued, "The human body can both contain, release, and demonstrate this absolute glory because it is wired to it. Its framework is created in this fashion to be able to hold it. It is the recognition of the ability to release it that is coming now to more saints.

"The flow of the vessel of the human body is designed to open its floodgates[21] and allow the release of the wavelength energy to manifest in the 3-D realm. This is what brings healing, body parts, revelation flow, vision, hearing, all spiritual senses, and the saints are also able to contain or modify the release of the flow of it."

You Can Steward the Glory

"What people first need to understand is that when they receive the presence of the glory, they are able to steward it. In younger, immature seasons, the receipt of the presence sent the human body into convulsions, rolling on the floor, or being slain in the spirit for hours. The matured sense of this is the ability to receive it and hold it like a vessel. This is your spirit instructing your body and your soul on how to steward this dimension of the wavelength frequency of absolute glory," he stated.

---

[21] The "floodgates" of a person is their mouth—their voice. A person can vocalize their agreement with Heaven via the words of their mouth.

Continuing, Joseph said, "In ancient days, there were humans so capable at this that they levitated off the ground. They were harnessing, holding, and containing the manifest absolute glory. Often, they did not have a way to release it to others, so they were holding it. They learned to hold it within their body. This is coming back into the earth realm.

The stewarding of the glory realm or the release of it to another is exactly that. It is for the purpose of the release to others that it comes.

The glory realm seeks vessels that it can fill, with the end goal being the release to others, not the capturing of it, holding onto it, or even measuring it out in small quantity. Glory looks for those vessels that it knows will be vessels filled to the point of overflowing, but will also release the overflowing," Joseph commented.

He continued his instruction by saying, "You can tell people that if you want more glory, you have to contract the trade of the release. It is a point or moment of agreement to receive and release for the purpose of manifesting the kingdom by bringing the needed resources. We must agree to be releasers of the glory. The recognition of the trade is that release.

The agreement to release glory means you get more glory—more of a manifest light of God, of Yahweh.

"Also, recognize that you can contain it, stewarding it well so that you can walk with it, talk with it, and move about with it. You are not seemingly unconscious on the floor with it. You are receiving it and stewarding it, but you are also releasing it in measured amounts where you are being directed to release it.

"You have both operated in this before," he mentioned, "and it's really nothing new, but **the amount and commonality of this is going to increase in days ahead**. It is going to increase first to those who want it, those who request it, and those who are learning. By that, I mean actively learning, focusing on the receipt, and then focusing on the release, wherever the release needs to go.

"You must:

- Want it.
- Request it.
- Learn to focus on the receipt of the glory.
- Focus on the release of the glory.

"This is going to surprise a good many demons and cause lots of screaming in the unseen realm," Joseph remarked with laughter.

He continued, "It is also going to awaken in people the understanding of the ultimate power of Yahweh—His love and His original intent of release. You call this giving of Himself.

"Heaven is enthralled with this component of Yahweh's character; He is always giving of Himself and He is always releasing of Himself. He is always abundantly more than you can think or know, releasing to you needed resources, opportunities, His goodness, and His nearness. His goodness is wrapped in His nearness."

All of this we had heard so far was simply the first thing he wanted to tell us.

He began again with more instruction. "Light particles carry this essence. Those operating in witchcraft and who have rebelled against the kingdom of God have sought to learn to control light particles in numerous ways through intellectual science and experimentation.

The Need for Protection

"The necessity of stewarding the release of the absolute kingdom glory must also come with the understanding of the need for angelic protection. This protection is not for you, the one releasing the glory, because the release of glory makes darkness flee. There will, however, be an intense work of darkness to spy this out and to intrude in deceptive or hidden ways, with the desired outcome being to capture what is being released to the saints.

"There are people who will be in danger when they try to do this **in an immature way, in a place of no alignment,** or **in a place where they've crossed out of their own boundary of authority** to engage in this. And by in danger, I mean their danger is to the kingdom of God itself, because the purpose of this Holy Spirit's activity is to increase the knowledge of the kingdom of God.

"Darkness will seek to spy out the land to discover ways they can capture it illegally. This would be an illegal trade, but they are going to seek it, nevertheless. They will fall under judgment for it, but until that day of judgment, the saints must be careful in practicing it. By practice, I mean their release of it. They must ensure that they have angelic forces forming shields around them to prevent illegal capture, theft, and general robbery as they learn to operate in this with greater efficiency."

Joseph continued, "This is what scripture is talking about when it says that some will be deceived. Even some of the elect will be deceived into believing that they are not being watched and studied by forces of darkness, thus the need for angelic activity around it."

Dialogue with Your Angel

"They need to learn to operate with their own angels in dialogue and communication so that they can gain help for their angels, as well as gain assistance from other ranks of angels, of which there are quite a few available. This is also so that the angels are there to ensure, at the saints' command, that nothing is lost or stolen from the kingdom of God."

At this point Donna became aware of textbook manuals being released. "Can I reach out and grab one?" she asked. She felt released to do so.

As she took one, Joseph explained, "They are releasing them for anyone who will receive the manual, which contains instruction, safety protocols, and utilization of His glory for purposes of the expansion of the kingdom of God. These manuals are actively being released into the earth now to any who will **choose to receive** and **verbally** bring them into their realm, the Father constantly giving and sharing with those whom He loves."

Immediately Donna pronounced, "I verbally bring it into my realm. I accept it and possess it, in Jesus' name. Thank you, Father."

A Green Light from Heaven

Joseph said, "There's a green light from Heaven on this and green means go! It is a re-introduction of this level of the release of His power as His sons and daughters on the earth access it. It is timed for this season, and it goes hand in hand with the work of angels as well as the revelation of angels, their ranks, their assistance, and how to navigate and collaborate with them for the increase of the kingdom of God."

"I have a question," Donna said. "You say that those involved with witchcraft and in league with darkness expect the saints to be able to operate in this more than the saints know that they even can operate in this, and they have already begun to spy this out for the purposes of theft and capture, right? It is like the saints are the last to know."

Joseph replied, "That is because the demon doctrines that have infiltrated the church have religiously limited people. The enemy is also not above using trauma, wounding, deception, or complete and outright bold-faced lies to teach people his doctrines, so that they are unaware. However, what is coming will change this because a remnant knows. Yahweh chooses to use a remnant to make known His power and glory wherever there is a need for resources on the earth."

"Just as you have taught others about their ability to come into realms of Heaven to request these needs be met," he remarked, "always remember you are releasing from *Heaven down* to the earth realm, and this is the design of Heaven—the perfect way. It is brought about like a waterfall out of Heaven through a window into earth, bringing necessary resources.

"Faith is required to open the window and make the request to send from Heaven down, and so it is with the release of this glory. Belief, understanding, practice, and the recognition of angelic forces at work to bring about the Word are all part of it. It is a frequency of light, but it has words. The release of it has words; words that are spirit language, words that are..."

Donna interrupted, "Oh, wow, the atmosphere is just full of words all of a sudden!"

Joseph continued, "It is definitely connected with vocal cords, vocal sound, words of language—meaning spirit language, words of command to angels, words of direction to the glory, words of release, and words of direction to the flow of Heaven. All these come by ultimate direction from Holy Spirit. The spiritually young will try to do this from their souls but directing the glory from the soul will never work. It is a spirit man activity. Many will be afraid to try or be captured by doubt, but there will be equally as many who will believe and begin this practice. This is going to change the 3-D world, because it will make the 3-D world like the kingdom of God, and it will all come through the saints.

God is going to manifest
His glory in this earth.
The earth cannot wait for this.

"Light wave particle energy is the rainbow. It is like opening your mouth and seeing a rainbow come out of it. That is what it looks like. Then the rainbow expands, and all the colors fill the space." At that moment Donna's office filled with the rainbow.

Joseph remarked, "You just saw the manifestation of it. What you saw was that the voice is tied to the release of the glory of God and the stewarding of the glory. Realize that when you do this under the unction of Holy Spirit, you are filling atmospheres with the substance of what would appear to you like the seven radiations (colors) of the rainbow, because the summation of that is the glory of God. That is why the glory of God will appear to you as bright, shining, white light—perfect, pure, and without blemish—what you would call blinding light. It is not for the purpose of evil, but for the purpose of everything that is right."

The Balance Scale

At this point in the engagement, an angel appeared carrying a scale not unlike our logo. It was a justice scale. Donna took it from the angel, and Joseph went on to explain its significance, "You must remember that the glory realm must always be released in perfect judgment. The justice scale you have received is a marker of righteousness and justice. It is a purity marker. It will always remain in balance when you are releasing the glory correctly. When you sense it is out of balance, you have likely moved to the soul realm and are no longer operating from the spirit realm. Your spirit knows when the scale is not even.

Justice is the foundation of His Kingdom. The redemption of all things out of alignment back into ordered alignment is justice.

The government of His Kingdom is justice balanced with the release of His power.

"You must have and operate in both. Operating without both leads you to rebellion, occult practice, witchcraft, illegal trade, broken barriers, and crossed boundaries.

"He is a God of justice. He is also a God of light and a God of giving. These three characteristics work in tandem for the expansion of His Kingdom in every realm."

"Father, I just thank you for that angel coming to bring that justice scale. I receive it and possess it in my realm. I ask angels to help me know its balance and I instruct my spirit to be aware of it and pay attention to it," Donna prayed.

Continuing, Joseph instructed, "God's justice scale brings a keenness of when things are out of balance, out of sync, or out of rightness. It brings the power to put it back into justice, justice being another way to say rightness. This is just the way light would do things, the way God would do things, the way Heaven and the seven radiations of God would do things."

Joseph said, "The seven radiations of God are going to be a sign in new ways. You are going to see it in new ways everywhere. You will see the sign of the seven radiations. Your spirit is going to be alert to this and you will know. Pay attention to the color you see in the spirit when you are in a moment of worship or prayer. It is going to direct you to what needs to be released."

"We are going to need more information about that," we realized.

He continued, "For now, just know that the seven radiations will become a greater sign in the earth in many expressions and manifestations in future days."

Donna interjected, speaking for both of us, "I receive that. In fact, I welcome that into the earth realm—the sign of Yahweh. We welcome the understanding of that."

With that, Joseph concluded his instructions. We, however, had some questions which he allowed us to ask.

"The seven radiations you mentioned that correlates to the colors of the rainbow?" I asked.

"Yes," he replied.

"It also relates to the seven spirits of God?" I continued.

"Yes," he patiently replied.

He expounded, "It also relates to the pouring out of the seven spirits of God in a new dimension of how you perceive and receive it. It is pouring out from within. Remember, from your belly will flow living water.

"It is related to this other phrase called the seven manifestations. The order of the seven radiations is their own linking together."

Donna could see, in vision form, these seven radiations. "I'm seeing them like a spirit being now, as well as where they take hold together and link together," Donna remarked.

Joseph enjoined, "It's always in the same order; that order is divine perfection. Its summation is absolute glory. The work of darkness is to twist that linking to gain a different light, an illegal light, and warp the manifested release to have to dominion over it or rule over it. The seven radiations are the light of God, the light God has always been. It is the eternal assets of the Godhead. It was the word—perfect agreement, perfect order. It is radiated light particles and release for expansion. It creates and it recreates. It orders and it reorders. It designs and redesigns. It positions and repositions.

"Some of this you simply cannot contain. Your spirit can garner a recognition of this, but the translation of it to the soul is muddied. It is somewhat beyond comprehension by the natural mind, but at the same time, it is so simple that a child could learn the wondrous wonders of Yahweh.

“The key to this is operating from the spirit, the freeing of the spirit, the awakening of the spirit, and the heightening of the spirits’ understanding of its own nuances. I’m talking about the human spirit indwelt by Holy Spirit,” he clarified. “The guidance of Holy Spirit and the receipt of Holy Spirit to possess all realms within your realm.”

Chapter 10
Things Are Beginning to Swing Open

On our latest journey into the riches of the realms of Heaven, our time started with a vision. Donna describes it in this manner: "When I stepped into Heaven, the first thing I saw was this big vision of a swing. It was the kind of swing that your grandfather would have made for you in the backyard, with a board and two ropes tied to a tree limb. It was a giant tree, a giant tree limb, and a swing. The swing was just going back and forth. It did not have anybody on it, but it was going back and forth, and I heard the word 'swing.'"

We sought more clarification on the meaning of the vision, and this was Heaven's response:

The Swing

The vision of the swing is a metaphor for things that are swinging open. A great many things are beginning to swing open, and the reason you saw the vision was so that you can bring hope to the people, both the people of your nation and the people of the nations of the earth who need to grasp hold of the hope that is contained within the phrase, "Things are beginning to swing open."

The natural world is going to receive the manifestation of the many things swinging open: open and shut, shut, and open, left to right, right to left. Many things that are on the wrong end of the spectrum will swing back to the other side of the spectrum. I am telling you this so that you can begin to grasp hold of the hope it brings. We have already administered through the hands of the angelic hosts the Oil of Hope. Now hearts need to hear the Word of the Lord:

"Things are swinging open."

They are swinging open for you. They are swinging open for your relatives. They are swinging open for your loved ones. They are swinging open for nations. They are swinging open for cities, counties, states, and provinces. This word comes to you that you may announce it from your physical flesh, releasing the frequency of Heaven pertaining to the swinging open.

Your spirit understands this better than your soul, and your spirit man can announce to your soul,

> *"Soul, announce this: 'Things are swinging open! Things are beginning to swing open. Let the swinging open begin. I agree with Heaven's announcement: things are swinging open. Things are swinging open for me. Things are swinging open for you. Things are swinging open for us. There is a great swinging open taking place.'"*

Next, Heaven instructed us to look up the definition of 'swing' in the natural. Here is the definition:

> *"swing - to cause to move vigorously through a wide arc or circle (//swing an ax); to cause to sway to and fro; to cause to turn on an axis; to cause to face or move in another direction (//swing the car into a side road"*[22]

Swing, or swinging, is an action. It is a verb. Swinging carries with it momentum of movement. Let the momentum of movement take place from your spirit.

Have your spirit translate it to your soul so that your soul begins to look for the manifestation of the swinging in order that you may glorify God. Let the swinging open appear. Let the swinging open occur. You can even declare, ***"My eyes will see this swinging open of a***

---

[22] "Swing." Merriam-Webster.com Dictionary, Merriam-Webster, https://www.merriam-webster.com/dictionary/swing. Accessed 18 Jan. 2021.

great many things." Heaven says the swinging—the swinging open—has begun.

This should bring a great deal of hope to your soul. This is what your soul has been looking for. It is the translation of the spiritual breath of God—His Word—from your spirit to your soul. Have your mouth say this:

> *"Awaken, soul, to the swinging open of what God has directed to open. Wake up to the swinging open that Yahweh has initiated. Open your eyes and look for the manifestation of the glory—of the King of glory—in the physical world. Wake up soul, hear the sound of the swinging open."*

As we continued our engagement, Heaven continued another topic.

Expectation of Harvest

During one engagement with Heaven, Lydia wanted to speak to us about a bag of seeds that we witnessed Ezekiel receive the prior day.

She began, "Many of you are aware of the phrase "seed time and harvest." Heaven wants to give you a new understanding of that phrase today.

A seed already comes with its harvest.

"A great many things have been seeded in prayer by the saints, and their faith is high that they will see an answer to their prayer. However, some prayers have been sown as seeds without the expectation of the harvest which that seed will bring. A lot of reasons exist for this. Many have been taught in the body of Christ that when you sow, you must wait a long time for the harvest. This is an incorrect teaching in the body of Christ. The truth of the matter is that a seed of prayer sown in faith (when the one praying has an expectation of triumph over time via supernatural conditions of power that are released by their faith) can come to fruition exceedingly quickly.

"When you pray, your prayer must be mixed with and spring *from* faith. Your prayer needs to be given wings of faith with not only sure expectation of answer, but within this hour with immediate expectation of an answer."

Lydia explained, "I am informing you so you can announce to those you know that when the expectation of quickly answered prayer is mixed with the sowing of the seed of prayer, the harvest of that prayer seed responds rapidly to the faith which it was sown, especially when it is sown quickly. Let me repeat that.

A prayer seed sown with quick expectation of an answer receives quick expectation of an answer!

"The belief of a quick answer is in this hour! I am not talking about yesterday. I am not talking about 10 years in the future. I am not talking about seasons from now. I am talking about in this hour, your prayer seed of faith needs to be for quick turnaround and a quick answer.

Quick harvest needs to be mixed with the fact that you expect to harvest quickly.

"When you sow the seed of prayer and expect a quick harvest, does the scripture not say that the harvester will overtake the plowman? (Amos 9:13) That is what I am talking about. The Father has made this available, but it falls to the saints to believe, teach, and share this belief—that *NOW* is when you can expect a quick harvest, much quicker than you have in seasons past. However, it will, as it has always done, rely on the faith of the one who prays *expecting that quick harvest.*"

She continued, "Formerly, the church understood that they had to pray with faith that eventually prayer would be answered, but now is the hour to pray for quick manifestation of the harvest, so begin to pray for this. Use the phrase,

---

"I am asking for a quick manifestation of the harvest. I sow this seed (this prayer seed) in faith with expectation of a quick harvest."

Release your expectation
for a supernatural harvest.

This is the instantaneous springing up
of the harvest the seed contained.

You need to view the seed
as if it carries the harvest
you are requesting.

"If you can see the harvest inside the prayer seed, release the prayer to the Father," she instructed. "Do this with the faith of expectation of that harvest and add to it the faith of *the expectation of a quick harvest.*"

Lydia elucidated, "Let me define the word 'quick' for you.

"Quick refers to the movement of Holy Spirit, where he can bring the answer with a swiftness that is due to:

- the increased number of angels which have been released onto planet earth,
- the greater number of people praying as one (remember, you do often need prayer agreement), and
- the timing for supernatural harvest.

"The timing of supernatural harvest is here, but how can the bride bring in the harvest if they have neither sent the prayer seed with expectation of a quick harvest, nor seen with confidence and assurance that their prayer seed *already contains their harvest.*

"Let me tell you plainly.

Your prayer seed already contains your harvest.

"See it and believe it. When you pray, are you seeing the answers to your prayer spring up in the realms of Heaven? If you can see this, all you need to do is invite angels to bring that harvest into manifestation in your realms and circumstances. You can now release angels to bring that harvest in a swift manner!

"I am talking about digging deep *within your soul to agree with your spirit* for the prayer seed that you have requested of the Father to manifest quickly.

You must have an agreement between soul and spirit for a quick manifestation of it.

"It is a prayer agreement between soul and spirit within your being," Lydia explained. "From this place, it generates hope for the harvest. Your soul becomes expectant to see your answer manifest, whether that is to see something right itself or straighten itself, to see a circumstance touched by God, or to see the supernatural overlay of the will of the King and His Kingdom come to pass. That is also what Jacob referred to in James 5:16 when he wrote that the effectual fervent prayer of a righteous man avails much. This kind of prayer is impacted by faith and expectancy. Expectancy energizes faith. Without expectancy, your faith is dead.

I caution you that this is for those who pray with Holy Spirit in maturity.

"The mature prayer of the sons of God mixed with *seed/harvest expectation* and *quickness of manifestation of that prayer* will see it come to pass quickly. You will see this!

"If you are aware that your soul does not believe this, you may repent to the Father and be forgiven, that you may.

Believe for quickness.

"The enemy has worked against this timing through false teaching, through resistance against faith within the body of Christ, and where previous manifestations did not occur quickly. 'We must forget what lies behind and press on to what lies ahead.'"[23]

---

[23] Philippians 3:13

She added, "If you need to repent to the Father for wallowing in the pit of despair due to lengthy delay of manifestations of answers to prayer, then do so. The Father holds no condemnation for you, and your repentance will help you exit the wallowing pit of despair. Then, get your soul healed in the presence of Yahweh, and through His love and healing angels, request a new awakening.

"Remember what Heaven said earlier.

Awaken your soul to possibility
so that your soul and your spirit
can agree for a quick manifestation
of the prayer of faith.

"I have mentioned before, and you've heard in the realms of God's Kingdom, that your abuse of your inheritance, which is the right to expect a quick manifestation of your prayer, *is simply a measure of having not heard Holy Spirit in prayer.* Some among you are like little children who are immature and:

- often pray from soul alone,
- have not mixed with their spirit in agreement, and
- in not hearing Holy Spirit, have set themselves up for much trouble.

"Now, the bride of Christ is growing up and in conjunction with Holy Spirit, she is learning to pray the will of the Father. These prayers are the object of our discussion here today. Now I am telling you—*mix in the expectation of quick manifestation.*"

She continued, "Heaven gently says, 'I know that you have many wounded among you regarding this topic.' Run into the strong tower of the Lord and receive your healing so that you will become the mature sons of God."

She finished by saying, "One last thing—by Holy Spirit's indwelling power within the members of the bride of Christ, the word 'quick' is a continuum. Think of the many expressions of Yahweh within the people of earth and within humanity. There are many varied definitions of the word 'quick', but when aligned with Holy Spirit, from their spirits these believers will have an ability to gauge the sense of the 'quick'. This is so they do not despair and give up hope but continue to mix faith.

"Let me tell you this clearly. The mixing of the expectation of your spirit and soul of quick manifestation is the avenue of trade from the heavenly realms which your Father wants to release in this time. Meditate from your spirit with Holy Spirit on the goodness of the Father in releasing quick manifestation. Do not take your eyes off His ability, His power, His kindness, His goodness, and the lengths to which he will go for His children."

Chapter 11

An Advanced Release of Joy

When we engaged Heaven another time, we heard these words:

"Things are picking up. Momentum is picking up for many.

"The advanced release of joy is needed.

Faith must shake hands with the expectation of joy for the momentum to continue to roll.

"Joy is an infusion into your realm and is based on the truth of the nature of God's character. Release an infusion of joy to your realm, to your ministry realm, verbally. It requires the words of your mouth. If you are unable to release an infusion of joy to your realm, it is because you have not invested time with your spirit realm bringing your spirit forward.

"Joy comes through the spirit. Joy is the spiritual component of His presence, and it comes from looking at and seeking after His nearness, His immediacy."

Heaven drew our attention to the Psalms:

> *You will show me the path of life; in Your presence is fullness of joy; at Your right hand are pleasures forevermore. (Psalms 16:11) (NJKV)*
>
> *For you bring me a continual revelation of resurrection life, the path to the bliss that brings me face-to-face with you. (Psalms 16:11) (TPT)*

"Nearness of joy is the result of drawing near to the Father," Heaven continued. "As a small child would crawl up into her daddy's lap, so you too can crawl onto your Father's lap. In that place of safety, you have not a care in the world. In that place of safety, you have contentment, bliss, and joy unspeakable.

"Nearness of joy can be received and passed to your soul. Your soul must be enlivened to joy. You must instruct your soul to cooperate with your spirit in the reception of joy to your soul's and body's realms. You can do this by the words of your mouth. Verbally announce joy to your realms—each of them that you know."

I announce joy to my spirit realm.

I announce joy to my soul realm.

I announce joy to my body realm.

I announce joy to my family realm.

I announce joy to my marriage's realm.

I announce joy to my ___________ realm.

Each realm must be a receptor of joy. It must receive it.

Heaven directed, "Whenever you have resistance to the reception of any of the fruit of the spirit to any of your realms, repentance may be necessary for believing that realm in question has the right to dominate from a carnal understanding. Call your understandings to yield to the truth of the Word of God and the truth coming from the realms of Heaven.

"As you allow your spirit to receive joy from the Father, it is not as if your soul is receiving the joy because it has limitations on how much it can receive. Your spirit has no limitations. Your spirit can receive joy without measure.

"Much worship is from the soul. It is not intended to be, but for many that is the case. When you realize your worship is from the soul, pause and call your spirit forward.

"The reverse action by which you have been living (soul-first) has caused you to judge first, then respond. Heaven would teach you to work differently as you learn to work from the realms of Heaven.

"When you teach your students to journal asking, 'What does Heaven have for me today?' they need to be doing that with their spirit forward because their soul will get tired. Their soul will consider it to be laborious and will discontinue doing the exercise after only a few days. Few will persist because working out of the soul is arduous.

"Many religious traditions have taught wrongly concerning joy and the reception of joy and the power of joy in the life of the believer. One such tradition says that if you request joy, you must wait a long time in the presence of the Father. That allows their soul to begin to dictate what happens in The Presence of the Father.

Pause in the present
to gain The Presence.

"It does not take long but it does take a pause," Heaven continued. "That does not mean that the Father delays from sending joy or granting joy to his children. He desires that his children walk in joy. Unless they walk in joy, they cannot walk in peace.

Joy is in the pause.

"Many have been wounded by having joy deferred. Yes, that is a thing, just like hope deferred is a thing. Much wounding has come because of joy being deferred. Again, that goes back to wrong teaching by the church. Request of the Father healing of the trauma to your being where your joy was deferred. For many it occurred in childhood and set the course of a lack of expectation or belief that you have an inheritance of joy.

"One such teaching is that your joy is dependent upon your circumstances. Joy that is from your spirit is never dependent upon circumstances.

> *Though the fig tree may not blossom, nor fruit be on the vines; though the labor of the olive may fail, and the fields yield no food; though the flock may be cut off from the fold, and there be no herd in the stalls— [18] Yet I will rejoice in the LORD, I will joy in the God of my salvation. [19] The LORD God is my strength; He will make my feet like deer's feet, and I will conquer by His song. (Habakkuk 3:17-19) (Septuagint)*

"Another such teaching is that joy must be earned. Another false teaching is that joy must be developed out of your discipline. Does not the Word say in Psalms that in my presence is fullness of *joy*[24] and at my right hand are *pleasures* for evermore?

"Joy is a secret for the healing hospital. You can request that joy be administered to the patient as the patient is receiving healing. A great part of the healing process involves the release of joy into the life of the believer—into the life of any person," Heaven expounded.

"Joy has been underestimated for its healing characteristics and how it can rejuvenate the body," Heaven continued. "Heaven wants the earth to

---

[24] Psalm 16:11

understand the power of joy and the benefits of joy in the life of a person.

"Joy is a presence, not a circumstance accounted from the hand of the Father. It comes at the request of the believer by the infusion of joy into that believer's life.

"Concerning the presence of religious traditions and how they have impacted the believer's belief system related to joy, repentance may be necessary for embracing false teaching and false understandings related to joy. If repentance is in order, simply repent. False teachings have kept many in bondage and out of touch with the nearness of the Father. The Father has always desired joy for his children, but religious traditions have said otherwise. The religious traditions are exactly that—traditions, and traditions of that nature always seek to invalidate and nullify the truth of the provision of the Father for His children.

"Simply cry out to the Father to forgive you of any embrace of false understandings concerning joy," Heaven instructed. "Ask that He would cleanse your heart, your mind, your entire being of the falsehoods you may have embraced. Many of these falsehoods were embraced unknowingly, but nevertheless, they were embraced. Ask the Father to erase all the old and wrong thought patterns of joy." Ask Him to give you new thoughts related to joy—new revelations and a new belief system to understand that joy is the expression of His delight in us. As we understand how the Father delights in us, joy will come forth. It is a part of the resurrection life we have been raised into.

Heaven continued, "Allow yourself time to let the delight of the Father refresh you. He delights in you more than you know or understand. His delight is not dependent upon your obedience, your sacrifice, or your manner of being. You need not seek His approval to experience His joy over you. You are His delight—His joy—His reason of bliss.

"The reason Heaven speaks to you of things like this is because you have need of joy now. Many of you went through seasons where you needed courage and boldness. You have received from the Father courage and boldness. You went through a season (and some of you are still in that season) where you needed hope. Hope has come.

"Now you are in the place where you need joy. It gives strength to your body. It causes you to rise when others around you are not rising. It causes you to extend your faith because of your conviction of the matchless provision of the Father for His children. He is not without concern for your or your situations. You may not have even considered that you needed joy, but your Father knew and has provided this avenue to stir up within you a fresh understanding of joy and what it can be and do for you.

"This season[25] can be for many a time of great sadness, but your Father has provided for you unspeakable, inexhaustible joy. You simply need to request from the Father the impartation of joy into your life—into your spirit," Heaven directed.

The Substance of Joy

The impartation continued, "The substance of joy comes from the presence of the Lord and is to be received and not emoted. It comes from the Spirit of the Lord connecting to the human spirit and is therefore not an emotion from the soul realm.

"The inclusion of the soul is good in the threefold body, but the soul cannot maintain the joy that the spirit can receive because the spirit receives constantly, like a river flowing in,[26] to fill the spirit realm with the joy of the Lord's presence. His Glory realm is meant to fill the spirits of humans with a seamless flow due to the unlocking of the cross.

"This feature is highly contested by the enemies of the Kingdom realm due to the oneness that is felt by the human in the release *and* receipt of joy from Kingdom realms. This is what the spirit pants for[27]—the joy presence of the One who is love, support, increase, and

---

[25] This was spoken to us in late November at the beginning of the holiday season.

[26] John 7:38

[27] Psalm 42:1

abundance, and the One who knows the depth of all things. As deep cries to deep,[28] the spirit knows its hunger for the presence of the Lord, and then translates the feeling of joy to the soul realm.

"The soul receives joy from the spirit when the spirit is present with The Presence as it acknowledges its' access and the opportunity to revel in God's glory.

"Why is this so? Because...

The spirit was created
to contain the glory of the Lord.

"This is what Satan is worried about—the sons of God recognizing their ability to carry his glory into every realm including the society of all mankind.

"It is the glory of the Lord that will be recognized by the spirits of all men," Heaven finished.

We asked, "Can you speak to us about announcing joy to our realm?"

Heaven answered, "The human spirit was created with the ability to recognize the glory of the Godhead and its connection to joy.

Joy is linked to glory
from the spirit side of humans.

---

[28] Psalm 42:7

“The place of closest spiritual union is the sharing of glory which translates to joy.

“When the angels announced to the shepherds, ‘Joy to the world,’ joy broke forth into the world through the birth of the Savior in both a prophetic announcement and a literal accomplishment: ‘Joy to your world; joy comes to your world.’ This is not an emotion. This is a substance of oneness in spirit form where humanity’s deficit was the spirit’s ability to receive joy from the glorious presence of the Father’s being—of who He is, of the I Am of I Am.

“Do you remember when Moses, with a shining face, came down off the mountain and they could not look at him? The reason for this is because his glory capacity to receive joy was so in effect that they tried to process that or translate that from the soul realm instead of their spirit, and it made the soul cringe or tremble. It made the soul feel its’ lack because the soul cannot process that spirit of joy-glory.[29]

“Spiritual joy, the joy that is in your spirit man, is a result of receiving the free gift of His presence—His desire to be one with His creation, His desire to be near, and His desire to be in His creation. This translates to your spirit as joy. Your human spirit must then translate this to your soul, but the soul has tried to manufacture joy for so long within humanity that it has lost sight of

---

[29] Joy-glory is the word Heaven used; it is explained later in this chapter.

the fact that it was never created to manufacture joy, but to appreciate the joy that comes from spiritual oneness, because the spirit is receiving joy from The Glory's nearness.

"This is why worship brings your spirit forward, but not worship that is demanded, nor worship that is required, but worship that comes from the soul's recognition of His glory, of the truth of His being: power, might, knowledge, wisdom, insight, ability, creativity—all things abundantly shared.

"The creation itself knows this glory and it is this glory that it longs for. At one time it knew The Glory. No wonder Jesus said, 'If you don't praise Me, the rocks themselves and the trees will cry out,'[30] because they recognize the glory in Jesus and the Father as the Creator, the origin of perfection of all things and it cries out for that. As the sons and daughters of God reveal the glory of His nearness and presence through their being—their spirit—creation itself will begin to respond," Heaven explained.

"What blocks this?" Heaven continued. "Because the enemy is afraid of this, what does he do? He shatters it with the soul and intellect. He attacks it with fear, abandonment, and rejection through all of this—through the employment of lies of your incapacity or inability to be who you were created to be—a vessel of the reflection of His Glory in oneness. The enemy cannot afford for you

---

[30] Luke 19:40

to think on these things and therefore he brings distraction, hard labor, and confinement (meaning confinement from other humans). You are experiencing this because there is something about how this joy from glory is transferable. It was on Moses, but you must receive it from your spirit man, not from your soul.

"Joy is attractive. People cannot wait to get into the kingdom of God through the Son because of the overwhelming amount of perception the soul gets from the recognition of the perfection of glory.

"Why do you think the Israelites followed the cloud—the pillar of cloud by day and fire by night? Because it was a release of the Father's glory into the physical realm and they could not help but follow Him. They were drawn to follow Him. Their hearts were aflame to follow Him and the spark of that flame came from the Passover. On earth you have the phrase 'men's hearts were aflame.'

"What is it that is trying to be expressed? The surrender to a greater glory in the things that represent the Godhead at that time—like the pillar of fire for the Israelites and in Jesus' day it is Himself and after the resurrection, it is His presence via Holy Spirit.

"On the road to Emmaus, their hearts burned (refined) within them as He spoke of Himself to them, unveiling to them His Glory. The hearts aflame were their spirits' reception of joy. It is the spirit's translation of joy to your soul.

"Do you not say, 'your heart burns within you?'" Heaven asked us. "You call it coals, coals for the seedbed of the joy link to His presence. The human spirit pants for this as it was evidently designed by God to do so.

"Another tactic of the enemy is to tamp down or shutter the spirit of the person through trauma or hardship. We might call this programming. Anything that brings the spirit of the man to the point of being broken, shattered, dysfunctional, or asleep is programming.

"This is the purpose of miracles. Miracles awaken the human spirit to its capacity to be filled with joy-glory. I am going to call it joy-glory for you because it necessitates The Presence to gain the substance of joy that is subsequently translated to your soul.

Your soul is meant to appreciate joy, not manufacture it.

"It is a spiritual dynamic of a human being to contain joy. Religious tradition squelches the human spirit from its capacity to receive The Presence because the human (and religious tradition) is self-oriented and it is do-oriented—like 'If I do this, if I accomplish this, if I measure up to this, I will have hope for joy.' However, that will never get you where you need to be because it is a spiritual dynamic of the Godhead and His Presence to give you the result of joy where your spirit translates to your soul that it is experiencing and appreciating joy."

Heaven instructed, "You really must work to change your mind, your words, and your thinking on this, because joy is not an emotion that your soul creates.

Joy is something that your spirit receives and translates to your soul.

"It is an appreciation of what has been given," Heaven declared.

We inquired, "When Paul said, 'Rejoice in the Lord, always, and again, I say, rejoice,'[31] can you unpack that just a little bit for us?"

Heaven answered, "This instruction was to keep your spirit buoyant. Another way to say this would be, 'Be in The Presence always,' and I say, again, 'Be in The Presence!'

EXERCISE:

When you see the word "Rejoice," replace it with "Be in the Presence"

"Jesus talked about Himself being the truth. 'I am the truth,' He said. Being in The Presence of truth is another avenue of being in The Presence of glory. Present your

---

[31] Philippians 4:4

spirit man to The Presence of truth. These two things are linked was what Paul was saying.

"Do you see that this is a (human) spirit forward direction and a presentation of one's spirit to be built within you? You must train your soul to cooperate with your spirit and take the subservient position. Present yourself to the Lord to be filled with His glory.

"When you just say the word glory, you are expressing that the Father's love has nuances. It is the perfection of the character of God. An expression of that whole can be presented to you where you are focusing or receiving one nuance of The Glory out of the whole. Your spirit picked up on the expression of glory known as love in that moment. It is a part of the whole thing called The Glory," Heaven explained, "but you could equally pick up on the expression of a fathering support or fathering protection or any of the finer nuances of the character of God and His overwhelming, never-ending, wide, deep, and concerned care for humanity and their expressions in this realm. God is always concerned, not to mean worried or anxious, but concerned about growing you into the best reflection of Himself which expands His Glory because the earth would be covered with the glory of the Lord, from sea to sea[32] in his people expressed outwardly. He is at work, working this out."

Heaven continued, "Do you see how your soul can rest? It can rest because the plan is in place. If your spirit

---

[32] Habakkuk 2:14

is following Holy Spirit, coached by Holy Spirit, taught by Him, led by Him, fed by Him, and curated by Him, then your vessel reflects Him to others and your soul becomes an agreeable steward of The Glory in seamless union with both your spirit and your body. In The Presence of His Glory, nothing wears out, so if your spirit man is receiving all His Glory on a consistent basis, your soul will be transformed to steward that glory to others in the physical plane, and your body will not wear out. It will be transformed by having been the physical carrier of the spiritual glory."

"Earlier we had a conversation about Cain, the son of Adam," Heaven reminded us. "Cain knew his physical body would suffer harm outside of the presence of the Lord.

"Satan seeks to find a way to corrupt the soul and the body using lies so that humanity cannot be the receptacle and the reflector of The Glory to the creation. He interferes because if humanity is this receptacle and reflector, he has no way to manipulate them with a lie or with his corrupting influence. He will corrupt the mind and the mind plays a part in locking down or shutting down the spirit. This is what Jesus was trying to tell the Pharisees.

The mind not renewed with truth
will close every door.

Heaven continued, "Jesus even said to them, 'You shut the door to those who follow you using their mind,'[33] which is not the use of their spirit. They closed the door to those who they were teaching to the access of who they really are in spirit-glory,[34] as receptacles, as disseminators, and as carriers of spirit-based joy."

Many of our conversations with Heaven began because we were wondering what to release to our CourtsNet students and our Mentoring Group[35] audience. The teaching in this chapter began because Heaven told us that a momentum is picking up and this momentum is future/present. It is in the present, but it becomes greater with faith and belief. The spirit man's panting after joy is a design motivator—as well as a divine motivator—to woo your spirit to the glory realm to be filled with joy.

Many of you are practicing on many levels what it means to be spiritual, what it means to have an activated spirit, and what it means to abide. From your spirit man, announce to your realms now the reception of joy.

Place a demand upon the release of His presence to your spirit and link your spirit to its desire to be filled.

It is all part of the process of being sons and daughters of God.

---

[33] Luke 11:52

[34] As sons of God learn how to live from The Glory, this expression outwardly is The Glory emanating from their spirit.

[35] Each Tuesday evening at 7:00 Eastern we conduct a free training via Zoom. Visit www.courtsofheavenwebinar.com to register.

What we, as a ministry, are helping people understand is their capacity not to look at the world, even though the world is all around you, but we are helping people understand the necessity for taking time to look to heavenly realms, to receive joy, truth, glory, and presence, for the soul and the body to be involved in the redemption process. We are teaching people a realignment, a new way, and a new season, although it really is not new; we just have not known to practice it. It is more like a broader season of availability of moving in this way as humanity. Heaven has opened this up to the Bride in this time.

Jesus did this continually in His life and His personhood—that is why He did what He did. His spirit was constantly being filled with the joy-glory; others call this bliss.

You cannot understand this if you think bliss is an emotion. We are not talking about an emotion, rather we are talking about a substance. We are talking about a receiving of a substance like joy or bliss.

Some people do not do this well, while others are teaching this too. We are just coming alongside to be our expression of this.

We asked Heaven, "Why would Heaven tell a ministry that trains in the Courts of Heaven about this topic?"

Heaven responded, "Because this is about transforming the mind to reach its capacity, to live from spirit first, to enjoy being in joy, and enjoy engaging Heaven. Numerous people are not enjoying it. Many are engaged in the Courts of Heaven, but they have not recognized their need for the enjoyment of the Courts, because in the enjoyment of the Courts of Heaven, you are not striving. You are moving with Holy Spirit. You are moving with The Presence. You are hearing a dialogue flow between both you and the one who is operating in the realms to bring a case in Heaven and who was helping you with the case. One should have joy in this, but many do not enter in with the expectation of joy in His Courts or His Presence because their mind is focusing on the political, the natural, the intellectual, and the legalistic. They are not engaging the joy in His courts and eventually your soul will squeeze off your desire to be in the Courts of Heaven.

"When you engage in Courts of Heaven paradigms of prayer, your spirit will receive joy because you are engaged in the realms of Heaven where His presence is continually—His goodness, kindness, love, support, help, abundance, perfection—all of these. If you are not coming out of your prayer paradigm in our Father's Courts with a sense of deep satisfaction, you are missing an element of what Jesus gave you."

Take a few moments right now and engage the presence of the Father. Receive the infusion of joy into your spirit so it can communicate this joy to your soul and body. ***Be in the Presence!***

Chapter 12

The Beauty of Gratefulness

As we tuned in one day to prepare for our Mentoring Group that night, we heard Heaven say, "The topic today is gratefulness. I know this is hackneyed at this time of year[36] for those in the United States, but I come to you to tell you: gratefulness is a key to unlock so many things have happened." Thus, began our engagement with Greg, a Man in White Linen. He continued, "Let me put it to you in this perspective. Here are some points about gratefulness:

- Gratefulness protects your humility.
- Gratefulness protects you from the Tree of the Knowledge of Good and Evil and its limited mindset, which forces structures of worldly capacities. Gratefulness begins to release you from its tendrils.

---

[36] This was spoken to us in late November 2020.

- Gratefulness is a recognition of your needs being met.
- Gratefulness protects you from mammon.
- Gratefulness forces the mindset of self and self-manufacturing of one's life and provision and it offloads that to the one who is capable—The Father.
- Gratefulness is an antidote for stress, especially when gratefulness involves one's humility.

Having a proper view

"We often see two sides of the same coin: Some see themselves as unworthy while some see themselves as too capable. A pendulum swing needs to land in the middle where you are both cognizant of your identity in Christ as an image bearer of Yahweh, but you are also cognitive that He is God and He alone," Greg stated.

My wife had a poster in an office where she worked that describe two principles of human enlightenment:

There is a God.

You are not Him.

When we understand those 2 principles, we reflect Him with a marked perfection because gratefulness is a part of our humility. I am not speaking of humility as viewing oneself as a worm, lying on the ground. Rather, I am speaking of humility as the accurate view of one's self. Humanity viewing themselves accurately elicits appropriate humility, considering the wondrous glory of God, His might, and His power offered through love. This is seen in the redemption story which Jesus both heralded and performed.

Greg continued, "Gratefulness as related to the Courts of Heaven is a key component of the ability to access the realms of Heaven, for when you feel unworthy, you do not go to the realms of Heaven and when you feel too full of self and self-idolatry, you will not go either. The medium ground is a narrow way as you are both kings and priests in the kingdom of Yahweh. Your knowledge of true humility increases your access to the realms of Heaven. This is a thing to be pondered.

Gratefulness is also linked to rest.

"Gratefulness is also linked to rest. As you are grateful, then rest can translate to the soul. Gratefulness is like a pool of refreshing. Command your spirit to spend time in the pool of refreshing called gratefulness. Your spirit is well able to translate this gratefulness and its rest to your soul. The problem comes when your soul is in front leading your life while you are trying to engage Heaven from the realm the soul knows—the natural, limited earth.

"But the spirit realm is full of gratefulness to others for the input of others into one's life and, of course, the accurate view of the love of the Creator to create for you the ability to live spirit first.

Your soul gains its rest from your spirit.

"All humanity needs practice in this. No one is doing it perfectly yet. Heaven has revealed this as a key to these times of uncertainty. One way to exercise this is to engage when your soul is at rest, your body is at rest, and your spirit is in the realms of Heaven, engaging gratefulness from this supernatural spiritual ground. From here, you can dialogue with many in the realms of Heaven to hear that which your spirit will agree with," Greg explained. "To be grateful for this kind of gratefulness is not solace; therefore, it is not keyed on emotion. It is keyed on fact and truth. It is keyed on the foundation of the perfection of the Father, His ways, and His timing. Your spirit connected to gratefulness in heavenly realms translates to the soul the direction it should take. If it is emotion, the soul is easily influenced and led astray by the natural senses. The realm of the natural is a successor of the unseen realm. Keep focusing on engaging into the unseen realm from the spirit through Jesus, the Christ.

"Engaging the gratefulness of His mind in the realms of Heaven gives you a truer sense of the gratefulness with which you praise God. The transaction of your spirit man, praising God from spiritual realms is unique and delightful. This opportunity comes to those who are maturing in Christ Jesus.

"A spiritual discipline is involved here. It is one that needs to be practiced because, at the beginning, you will find that you are not very good at it, but the more you engage gratefulness from the spiritual realm, the more at rest your soul will be. Much of this is like breaking the mold of the mind of your soul—the mind of your flesh—into new thought patterns, allowing your thought patterns to come from the truths that are in the spirit realm," Greg clarified.

The foundational principle of worshiping God in spirit and truth must be done from the spirit realm.

It must be done spirit first. It must be done from the spirit's access to the spiritual realm, translated or transferred down to the soul. Our understanding of this is linear, but the more time we spend in the heavenly realms, the less linear our thinking becomes, and the more possibility is translated from the spirit to our soul.

Our soul is designed to delight in this as it receives the creativeness of the realms of Heaven and our spirit is teaching our soul its true ability. It is teaching our whole being new truths from which to live life.

Unlocking Rest

Gratefulness is key to unlocking rest, experiencing the nearness of His presence, and even creativity within the soul.

Try it sometime.

If you are feeling closed off or shut down in creativity, the pathway of gratefulness from the heavenly realm—the spiritual realm, the Kingdom realm—begins to unlock you. It unlocks the soul's stress. The reason I say to practice is because practice involves a choice and intent.

Unlocking Joy

Greg added, "Another thing that gratefulness will unlock is the joy of Heaven to be translated to the soul. It is like eating from the Tree of Life. Focus your spirit eyes on the goodness, abundance, and pleasure of your eternal destiny in Jesus. Do not take on the burdens of life that have not been given to you by the Father but have been elicited within your soul by the deceptions of the adversary. Release them to the Lord and engage in the delight of your spirit's access to heavenly realms. From this vantage point, your gratefulness becomes shiny. It becomes a treasure.

"One thing that will stop you enjoying this access that Jesus opened is allowing the soul to think that it is the lead to correct, fix, and bring into perfection the earth realm. This is completely wrong, as it will only come through the spirit—the spirit of the believers, the spirit of mankind in Jesus, the spirit which contains the mind of Christ by the power of Holy Spirit indwelling in humanity. This spirit translates these things. If your soul is trying to be grateful, it can only get so far because it feels the burdens of life, but your spirit feels the joy of Heaven and knows the Tree of Life. Only from Heaven down will true gratefulness translate back to your soul. Creativity, rest, and joy arise again.

"When you are comparing yourself with others, instead of comparing yourself with yourself, you set yourself up for getting stuck. It is only the Father who knows all things of every heart; therefore, your comparison of your circumstance with another person's circumstances will never hold true because you do not know all things. The spirit does not need this comparison. Therefore, as you are engaged in spiritual realms, you can receive the things that make the soul at rest, gain creativity, and contain joy. When your soul is in front of your spirit, these things are hampered.

"The conclusion that the soul draws is often clouded by untruth, and the soul feels burdened without the access to be the spirit being you are created to be—as one who holds the breadth of Yahweh. The soul has typically operated independently of your spirit and has yet to learn this new dynamic and way of living. Your joy comes from recognizing how close spiritual things are to you. As you have been awakened in Jesus, you are acknowledging His kingship, Lordship, victory, angel armies, and counsel as from one who knows all things. This is the pleasure of Heaven in the presence of the Father and is made available to the saints upon the earth.

"This is an area of new awakening and reawakening of the spirit man.

"Your spirit hungers to be grateful, but not as the kind of grateful that is led by the soul; rather, it desires to be experienced in Heaven among the atmosphere of true gratefulness in the Heavenlies, in the unseen spiritual realm of Heaven. Gratefulness is a pervasive aroma, and it contains rest as well as joy. This manifest as you acknowledge that all things come from the Father who is a good giver and has provided well for all that is needed.

"The soul demands its contemplations[37] and this is mostly true because the soul has been given reign over the flesh and the spirit. However, when it is in its proper place, and the seamless beauty of spirit, soul, and body are at work, the spirit can then translate to the soul the winds, breath, and refreshing of Heaven, the soul becomes at rest and the being of that person is made well and whole and they find wholeness and oneness."

"It is rather a mystery that I am explaining to you," Greg continued, "but the reason we use the word mystery is because it is something that must be sought out. It must be dug out. It must be uncovered. It must be mined. It must be found, and it is not found in the 3-D plane—rather, the spirit plane is the greater dimension, and so it is found in this plane. It is the reawakening to what Jesus opened as the last Adam so that the sons of

---

[37] The soul wants to examine everything it does not understand. Then it wants to be able to give it approval before you engage in a new activity. It has operated outside of Heaven's desire and design.

God can become true sons and daughters of the Most High reflecting His peace, His glory, and His perfection.

"This is a good thing to remember as some families are meeting and some families are not meeting and some have forgotten what the cultural holiday is about in lieu of the burdens of the day, but the key to that is a spiritual ascension and engagement with Heaven.

"I do not want to overburden you. Rather, I want to leave you with hope," Greg explained. "I want to leave this with you as a reminder to access this joy. I want to leave you with this challenge: that the peace you seek for and the true definition of gratefulness is a Heaven down concept. This is kind of like re-introducing spirituality back to a cultural holiday that has become completely culturally bound."

Continuing, he reminded us, "Here is what Jesus did to let His being 'catch-up' as He lived in the flesh with a soul: from His spirit, He sought out solitude for catch-up time. He allowed himself to be ministered to by the love of the Father."

In our day, the dispute is over our ability to find solitude from distraction and to be in the presence of God. It is a territory that is disputed or contested for by darkness. However, the Father is not anxious whether that His sons and daughters will not come to Him for refreshing, because he is doing a work in His children and He knows that they will learn rest.

Sometimes the 3-D world in which we live will be in our face. It will be so in our face that we will need to rise early or go to bed late, having carved out a short time for solitude in His presence.

Take time to embrace His presence.

Chapter 13

Accessing Rest

Malcom began with a series of questions. He asked, "Have you found yourself weary? Have you been asking, "What makes me weary with all this?" or, "What is pulling on me that makes me weary?"

"You are not alone," he answered for us, "the demands of the season, the demands of the current pandemic, simply the demands of life can make us weary and in need of respite. Thus Malcolm[38] began this episode of our engagement with Heaven. He noted a few things that make us weary and how to overcome the weariness.

- Do not try to live another person's life.
- Do not try to do another's assignment.

---

[38] Malcolm is a Man in White Linen who often teaches us in the realms of Heaven. He is also the Headmaster for our CourtsNet program.

Malcolm continued, "When you do not come to the Father for rest for your soul, that makes you weary.

You must come to the Father for a rest for your soul and you must make time to pause just to be.

- As you pause just to be, *you must be in the present*. He made you that way. He designed human to be in the present in time. If you are living too far in the future, or if you are living too far in the past, you are not present in the present.
- *You must limit distractions*. First, you must discern them and then you must do the work of limiting them. You have authority to limit distractions. Everyone does, but people do not recognize it in a world filled with distractions.

Rest is for the soul.

"Your soul craves rest, was designed for rest and lost rest by the corruption received through the corruption of the identity, the human being, and the three-part human. The Savior redeemed the three-part being of humans back to its rest. Jesus redeemed us back to rest so that the soul is encased in rest.

"Think of rest like a garment you could put on or like a case in the natural. You carry things in a case. You put an object in a case. Sometimes you buckle it, snap it, or zip it, but it is encased.

Your soul is meant to be
encased in the rest of the Father.

"When encased in rest, your soul is content. Contentment and rest are similar.

The problem has been that your soul
is striving to achieve contentment
instead of receiving the spiritual
quality of rest and contentment
from the Father.

"Rest is a component of being a son of God. A son or daughter's rest is a component of a relationship with the Father, Son, and Holy Spirit. The soul agrees with the creativity of the spirit when encased in its rest. In the physical realm, the soul also hunts for peace, but peace cannot be found for most from the physical realm in its current state under the usurper. There will come a day when the physical realm is returned to the full measure of peace, but that is not today.

However, human beings
are designed for peace.

"Humans hunger after peace. Therefore, Heaven and the presence of God causes the soul to rest and the spirit to be awakened and enlightened.

"When Jesus walked the earth and the people pressed in around Him, what do you think they were pressing in for? Why were they pressing in? Was it for the words? Was it for the healing?" Malcolm asked us. "Primarily it was for the peace that he exuded—the frequency of peace that they hungered after that they could not find anywhere else in their day, certainly not from religious leaders nor from the work of their hands.

"This peace is a quality deeper than calm. It is richer than happiness. It is more lasting than life. Peace is a quality of Heaven that gives us equanimity (calmness), balance, and joy. Human beings were created to excel and designed to linger in the presence of peace and rest that the soul needs, for the soul is primarily at rest in the presence of peace.

Engaging Heaven

"Your enemy, the one who vexes all humanity, is a thief of rest to your soul and its consequent peace. Engaging with the realms of Heaven enables your soul to rest as your spirit comes forward to partake of that substance of Heaven with which it delights. This new way of life is so opposite the physical realm under the rulership of the usurper that the intellect despairs at its inability to achieve it. However, provision and portion has been made for God's sons and daughters to receive rest in their soul that they may be the portals and outlets of His Kingdom on earth," Malcolm clarified.

Entering the Rest of God

Labor to enter into my rest. (Hebrews 4:11)

"The working out of this scripture in your day is the access to the realms of Heaven that has been opened on to you and to the nuances of learned activity that your spirit knows to engage with Heaven in new ways," Malcolm stated. "Primarily, this is what we teach and help others to understand, and when they comprehend this, it helps them become free from other captivities so now they are enabled to engage the enlargement of their spirit. As the spirit man of a human is enlarged with oneness with the Father, the soul sighs with relief due to its recognition of how corrupted its life has been with any other alignment.

The Equation of Time

"I will tell you a mystery. The time of operating in your spirit does not compare one-to-one with the time in the physical realm. Time spent in Heaven is much more multiplied to your soul and therefore is not a one-to-one ratio. One minute spent in the realms of Heaven does not equal one minute spent in the physical realm, engaging the physical realm with your soul, which—by the way—was what it was meant to do. Your spirit was the first to receive the rest that your spirit knows as your rest engages with Heaven and the presence of God. It then transmitted that to your soul. A short time spent in the realms of Heaven engaging with spiritual things equates to a multiplication of many more things, many more minutes of rest that the soul receives, your spirit having engaged Heaven and the beauty of the things found in this dimension.

"Does the scripture not say that before Adam and Eve ate of the wrong tree, 'They walked with God in the cool of the day'? This engagement with their spirit in the presence of the Lord equated to their physical ability to operate from rest to carry out assignments and duties in the physical plane.

"The soul in front of the spirit feels anxiety and worry about these things.

The spirit in front of the soul causes the soul to rest.

"After having engaged in spiritual activity in the realms of Heaven by worship, by receiving, by surrendering, by positioning one's spirit to be at the forefront to be loved by the love of Heaven—only then will these things translate to the soul that the spirit may continue in these places. Then in your daily life, on the physical plane, if you operate from what you have engaged in, it will go well with you," Malcolm explained.

He continued, "Now I am going to talk to you about the Courts of Heaven from this paradigm. Do not strive to enter the Courts of Heaven. Striving in the Courts of Heaven causes many court cases to go awry and not receive a resolution due to people entering the courts with striving or worse, with manipulation upon their heart. They feel stymied in the courts because they have entered in wrongly.

"Would it not be better to come into the Courts of Heaven as you enter in to approach from a more spiritual dynamic with your soul at rest?

"Remember, you are told to enter in with praise and thanksgiving[39]. I am to tell you to first partake, and I really mean partake, of the beauty of Heaven first before going to the courts. Partake of the presence, partake of the spirit of hope, partake of the seven-fold spirit within your spirit. Come first to receive before you go into the courtroom to do court work or to bring the case that you have upon your heart to bring before the Lord. Many things become easier when you enter in this way," Malcolm explained. "This is an alignment, and all things in Heaven are perfectly aligned, so as you step into Heaven, take time to get aligned. From your alignment, your positioning and work in the Courts of Heaven will begin to flow more smoothly.

---

[39] Psalm 100:4

The soul that strives
does no one any favors.

"The soul must be at rest to gain the ultimate benefit of what you have been given access to. Your spirit knows the difference when you have entered in with striving on your heart—striving as in labor, hard work, self-work, self-presentation, or self-preservation. Your spirit comes here to receive because preservation for you is already here. It is in you. It is in the plan of God for you to receive, not strive after as a thing to get, but as a thing to position oneself to receive. This is a nuance of the work of your spirit in conjunction with Holy Spirit. Holy Spirit is stepping into spiritual realms with you because you are one and are united with Him, whether you are aware of Him or not. His desire to help you in this realm comes when you position yourself to receive Him and receive what Jesus gave you access to.

Limiting Distractions

"One more thing: your understanding about your ability to limit distractions is a paradigm shift for many.

Your role in earth's realms
is to rule over distractions as if
you are the king of that realm.

"This is because, in a sense, you are king of that realm because He lives in you. You must take rulership over the distractions of the world so that you are not conformed to its manner. People who take this ability and calling to limit distractions in their life will be ridiculed and persecuted by the world. Why? Because the world has lost its hold on them." Malcolm instructed, "Ridicule and persecution from the mouths of those the enemy would use will come against you because you found a better way, and therefore, the world has lost its hold on you. It has lost its grip, its position as a slave master. When you think of distractions in these terms, you begin to get a deeper sense of living from Heaven down under the calling, identity, and assignment that the books of Heaven contain about you. It is a choice, but isn't He worth it?"

Chapter 14

Dealing with Hope Deferred

As we engaged Heaven one day for instructions concerning the upcoming Platinum Members meeting that we hold weekly, Heaven gave us some insights. We were told that some would come with questions, some with testimonies, and some with struggles who simply needed to be reminded to return the burden to the Savior, Lord Jesus. Some were coming who were feeling weary and needed a refreshing from the pool, and still others who were feeling weary because the journey was longer than expected and their hope was diminished.

In Amos 9:11, we read, “An enemy will be all around your land, he will sap your strength from you and plunder your palaces.” This scripture outlines the goal of the enemy, which is to plunder your life. One of the ways he does this is to attack your hope. When you become weary, it is because your soul is having its say and it results in your heart feeling weary. Here, the heart is being subjected to the opinions of your soul.

The Father desires for hope to reside in the hearts of each of His children. One way we can receive that is to allow angels, with the assistance of hope, to minister to the beliefs caused by hope deferred. When God is saying, "You can!" hope deferred may be saying, "It will never happen!"

Heaven pointed out to us that another way this is handled is to repent for hope deferred, or for embracing hope deferred and what it said once you embraced it.

You may be unaware that your hope came alongside hope deferred and is now seen through that lens rather than the lens of hope. You must intentionally come out of agreement with hope deferred and redirect your heart to receive hope. You may need to refresh yourself by reading promises from the Word that stir up hope within you. Once you do this, you stand to receive every refreshing that ministering angels can bring to you. This is the activity of the sons of God in Jesus.

You operate with Holy Spirit, allowing the course of your heart to be redirected by Him. Courtroom repentance and confession for being distracted and waylaid by the belief system of hope deferred is helpful as well. Not everyone needs this, but I am giving you ways to leave behind hope deferred and focus your heart and eyesight forward to hope in Christ Jesus.

Sometimes hope deferred shakes hands with the spirit of fear. Confession, repentance, and requesting cleansing from that defilement, combined with the request that angelic realms be released to bind and remove the spirit of fear from one's realm is equally helpful.

After confession, repentance, and requesting the atoning blood to cover one's self, you need to command the spirit of fear to leave now, as it has no legal ground upon the heart any longer. This also is helpful.

These ways to freedom will help the spirit to feel buoyant once again and bring clarity to the soul.

The knowledge that it is not necessary to live within the constraints placed by fear or by hope deferred is liberating. The soul must move to spirit first. God is gracious in this and Holy Spirit will assist. It is a collaborative work within your being to agree with the truth of Yahweh, and it often requires you to pause for a moment to accomplish this.

The Communion Table

The communion table is laid out for you as a remembrance of your ability in Jesus to achieve this state of hope. Communion in the physical realm is helpful as your body, soul, and spirit merge in heartfelt understanding of the significance of communion.

Recall that Jesus is the lifespring within you. His DNA and blood, in essence, replace your own DNA and blood as you engage in communion and its remembrance of covenant level sanctification. This makes the enemy tremble, and you become less of a target because the flame of God within you is released at greater intensity.

I want to remind you that you are amazing creations in Christ Jesus. What is being developed and done in these days will be seen by the nations and the world and its structures. Thrones of iniquity will begin to be weakened. This is the army of Yahweh, His sons and daughters accomplishing their destiny on earth with Him at their side.

Chapter 15

Accessing the Strategy Room

Recently, Donna and I accessed Heaven to find out what Heaven's agenda was for that day. We already had a hint of what we would be doing because, on the prior day, Ezekiel mentioned a phrase in passing that seemed to point to an upcoming engagement. On this day, we were told to visit the Strategy Room with Lydia.

The Strategy Room is not part of the Business Complex, but simply an aspect of the realms of Heaven. It is more than just a room; it is a whole department. It seemed to take up an entire wing of a large building. Lydia was with us, and once we were in the Strategy Room, she walked over to the wall, opened a drawer, and pulled out a file and a device that was a projector of some sort.

As she put the device on the table in front of us, it presented a holographic image in 3-D. The image represented the sphere of LifeSpring International Ministries. The sphere itself was intersected by tunnels.

Lydia informed us that a lot of information could be gained from the Strategy Room and from this holographic image. She advised us that what goes on in the Strategy Room that we have access to also involves others who work in the room, including some from the cloud of witnesses. They or their work comes in here and they can keep tabs on what is going on.

Ezekiel notified us that he had been in this room before and had talked with others about LifeSpring. We were told a lot goes on behind the scenes.

Just prior to our engagement with Lydia and the Strategy Room, we had met with Ezekiel to discover what he needed that day. From that encounter, Donna had the following question, "When Ezekiel asks us for booby traps,[40] is it on his own or is it coming from here?"

We learned that this is the room where we can come to access the booby traps. In the intricacies of the heavenly realms, it is all interconnected and so, in our situation, Ezekiel has angelic knowledge of what is needed we were told. He explained, "This comes from his connection through this Strategy Room on behalf of the ministry because of who we are, what we are doing, what

---

[40] Booby traps are an angelic weapon not unlike IED's (Improvised Explosive Devices) that our military is familiar with now.

our trade is, and how we are organized. A seamless background work is in place on our behalf."

"This department is interested in keeping you off the radar of the enemy. It releases to those who work on your behalf what they need to know and what their background work is on your behalf. These are angels and cloud of witness people (the great cloud of witnesses).

"You can come here to learn about any new thing of which you need to be aware. Lydia advised us that it would be good for her to accompany us when we come to the Strategy Room so she could explain things to us.

"The tunnels that were seen intersecting through the sphere of LifeSpring are the dimensional travel pathways of the angels of God on assignment."

[Ezekiel was to be commended for the patrol of these tunnels, as well as patrolling the boundaries of the sphere. His work was to create strategic tunnels (we might call them wormholes) through which angels could come and go on behalf of LifeSpring. It allows them to work with speed, delivering things like bonds and traveling with a certain amount of covertness against the enemy.]

Heaven recognizes timing as well as excellence, and always has the intent of surprising the enemy with a display of threat and power regarding the enemy's coming demise and defeated status."

"Now that we are here and both of you hinted that we had a reason to come, what is the reason? What else is there to do here?" we inquired.

In response, Donna began to see what looked like a topographical map. This, too, was a representation of LifeSpring. She could see the borders, and although this was a different perspective, she could see on this map fires that were set by the enemy which had been put out, representing enemy attacks. She could also see, highlighted on the map in a color-coded key, the current works of darkness against what we as a ministry are trading on.[41]

The color key uses the colors of the rainbow and yellows, reds, and oranges are where there is fierce activity against what we are doing. When looking at the map, she could see Ezekiel had been doing a good job, because she only saw one or two little hotspots, which was not much at all compared to the enormity of the space on the map.

Then she noticed that the map had an overlay. She could touch a button, and the map showed an overlay of time, allowing her to look at the past, where she saw a lot more yellow, red, and orange. When she looked at the present, it looked quite good, much better than it had looked a few weeks before.

---

[41] Trades and trading floors are discussed more thoroughly in the chapter on "Trade Routes."

“Can we look at the future?” we asked.

This made Ezekiel laugh. We noticed they were not answering that question. The reason for not answering was simple, they explained. It is because it is by faith and faith changes the future. Based on your faith, the future is still being worked out. That makes faith important, as it always is. “Faith is what we are all operating on,” they said.

Donna noted what she had been seeing the last few moments and shared what she was hearing. “I have been seeing rope and I just heard the word ‘lariat’ from Holy Spirit,” she remarked. Holy Spirit was helping us understand that the strategy and weaponry needed by Ezekiel and his ranks were rope and a lariat. We were told we could request these for Ezekiel and his ranks. They cautioned us to remember that this rope was not made from materials of earth but made from materials of Heaven. This rope is powerful. It is released to capture and bind, and it is not easily broken.

Donna realized that simply by standing in the Strategy Room, she did not have to know a lot of things. She could wait to be shown something and then make the request on our angels’ behalf.

“Do we just make that request or is there a court you need to access?” we asked.

“You will know the difference when you are in the Strategy Room,” we were told. Further clarity was given, “You will know whether you need to go to the Court of

Angels and request it there, or just request that the Father give it to your angel. This is a function of how practiced you are in the realms of Heaven. Now, ask of the Father for your angel."

"Father we ask for our angel rope and lariat from your storehouses," we requested.

Ezekiel informed us that the Strategy Room is a place we could come when he was not coming directly to us to request things.

[At times we had called our angel near and he did not immediately appear. The answer was simple. He was busy. Now, with this information, we knew what one of our options were. We could wait on him to appear or we could access the Strategy Room, find out what he needed, and petition for those things on his behalf without him ever being present.]

The Anchor

As we proceeded, Donna realized she was seeing something else—a large anchor. Ezekiel told us that the anchor, together with the rope, was another tool for their use. They use it to tether demons, so their movement is restricted, much like anchors in the physical world prevent free movement. Demons hate anchors.

In response to this, we requested anchors of the Father for Ezekiel, his commanders, and his ranks. We also commended them to the Father for the excellent way they use the anchors which limit and restrict activity of realms of darkness. We also commended them for their effective manning and patrolling of the tunnels on behalf of the ministry.

Chaos Net

Next, a large net was seen. It seemed exceptionally fine in its construction, and it had weights all around it. It was a large circle, taller than Ezekiel. Ezekiel referred to it as a Chaos Net. He explained that he uses it to capture chaos.

"It expands in such a way that you can put it over an atmosphere, and it will trap the work of chaos," he explained. We had needed that.

Request of the Father for Your Angel

We requested of the Father, on behalf of LifeSpring International Ministries, that Ezekiel, his commanders, and his ranks would be provisioned with Chaos Nets to trap the chaos in the atmospheres of all those who are aligned with LifeSpring International Ministries. We asked this in Jesus' name.

Chaos, Intimidation & Distraction

Lydia was smiling and remarked, "This is the good work of the saints, to co-labor with the angelic for the capture of every hindrance, limitation, and defeat, which leads to the utter defeat of realms of darkness." She explained that **the amount of chaos in the nations right now is the number one tool of the enemy**, along with **intimidation and distraction**.

The net could be small, or it could be as big as a city. Angels secure it. It can be secured over a business, a realm, a person, a city, or even over a nation. It works somewhat like the shields of the earth. It contains the power of God for the destruction and shutting down of the work of chaos.

Agree with the Angel & Commission Them

Once the Chaos Net has been requested, tell your angel that you agree with him or her. Commission them to release the Chaos Nets to trap and limit all works of darkness operating in confusion and chaos throughout your realm, wherever needed.

In faith, agree with your angels work that these Chaos Nets are effective and that they are mighty unto God even for the pulling down strongholds.

Fill the Void with Peace

Once you remove chaos from an atmosphere, remember that where something has been removed, it must be replaced. The request of the **release of bonds** does this, as well as **commissioning your angels to**

work and bring peace. The decrees of the saints ensure that these things can settle in as the chaos is removed. This enables Heaven to work in that situation. It also allows people to receive the goodness of what is coming through the prayers of the saints and as people release bonds and pray for each other.

Limitations of Use

One thing to note about the Chaos Nets is that *your authority to use them is related to your degree of authority.* For instance, if you were to request of the Father that your personal angel be armed with a Chaos Nets, her ability to use that would only touch your personal realm. If you have authority in a larger realm, it can touch that realm.

At the same time, if you are part of the United States, you could request for the angels assigned to Union[42] to use the Chaos Nets. However, you must remember that its use is based on one's authority level. It is a form of agreement that the angels can use the Chaos Net over the nation.

In places or states where you have no ties except for friendships, you do not have much authority. Therefore, you cannot ask the angels of that area or state to use the Chaos Net to remove chaos. There are many other ways

---

[42] Union is the chief angel over the United States of America. Dominion is the chief angel over Canada.

to pray but understand there are limits. Do not get outside your boundary. It is important to work with Heaven rather than out of ignorance or spiritual immaturity. Just as you would not give the car keys to a two-year old, Heaven will not entrust you with more authority than you can handle.

"Could we request revelation of these weapons for the intercessors responsible for the nation?" we wondered.

"You could, but it would be wise to start with your own nation's intercessors to request they receive revelation of the weapons available to the angels as well as their use. You could even start by sharing and teaching this understanding to your own intercessors or other intercessory groups the ministry may align with."

Intimidation

We inquired, "Are there weapons like intimidation and distraction? "

Ezekiel replied, "You meet like with like, so with intimidation, you would arm your angels with weapons that intimidate."

Recently, Ezekiel requested cannons. Cannons are large weapons that are an effective threat deterrent. The realm of darkness uses show of force to intimidate, and by loosing cannons to our angels, they can use them to meet intimidation with greater intimidation.

The Tool of Distraction

"Distraction is a favorite tool of Satan because he says, 'Look here, not there,' Ezekiel explained. "He will distract you by pulling your gaze in one direction, so you are not paying attention when he is in another place doing a dirty deed. When he manages to turn your gaze, it enables him to pull his stunt."

"What is the comeback for distraction?" we asked.

Ezekiel replied, "Weapons of clarity and vision, such as magnifying glasses, binoculars, or goggles of various types, are angelic weapons. In the co-partnering relationship, the saint praying for these weapons to be used by the angelic guard creates a link which brings clarity to the saints when these weapons are used by the angelic."

When angels are using these weapons, we feel the result and can stay more focused. Focus is defined by letting the main thing be the main thing and not letting the minor things take precedence.

In realms of prayer, the saints often touch on this through tongues, fasted states, and visions that they are given. These are instances of openings of spiritual realms of clarity that the saints agree with and pray and speak into.

Since distraction is a common tool of the enemy, request of the Father the arming of angelic hosts. According to your authority and your boundary, ask that the angels be given these weapons, although they are not weapons in the typical sense, not like a gun or arrow. It simply benefits us.

Ezekiel explained, "When exploring the Strategy Room, do not get too wrapped around the axle on this. Angels have many weapons that you will never know of, but we still employ them despite that."

"What else do you have to show us here?" we inquired.

Lydia answered, "We are just about done here. Be sensitive to this place when you check in to the Help Desk, whether in the Business Complex or the regular Heaven's Help Desk."

She explained, "In prayer you can also come in here. If you have a problem which needs strategy, realize that strategy is linked with warfare, but strategy is also linked with justice, meaning the working out of justice. In most cases, the saints will use it with those two motivators to war against the enemy and to bring justice."

Employed by Angels

Lydia continued, "We can come to the Strategy Room to *gain* strategy, but we *employ* the strategy through angels. In contrast, in the courts we utilize the counsel of the court, Holy Spirit, and men and women in white linen to give us understanding of how to legally bring something about. The Strategy Room is linked with more direct angelic activity than the courts.

That may not sound like a true statement because both operate with angels, but if you stop at the Help Desk, you will know when you need to be here. Do not worry about it unless you are told to come but recognize the need to come to heavenly realms to find out."

She concluded, "Remember, it is all linked. Heaven is a communicative place. Beings in Heaven all operate together in a unity that we do not have in the earth realm. It is vastly different in Heaven. You will discover links between revelation and strategy. It is very graded. It has many layers of different things. You may ask, 'What strategy do we need for this thing?' You may discover you do not really need strategy or the same level of strategy for another thing. A different level of strategy may be needed. Humans often work on these things in prayer without realizing that is what they are doing. It seems to humans to simply be revelation."

Chapter 16
Shields of Protection

Lucas, a Man in White Linen, met us one morning to teach us about veils, also known as shields. We went to the Place of Receiving, which felt like a classroom of sorts.

Lucas began, "I am here to give you a linear explanation of veils, otherwise known as shields. You must free yourself of earthbound thinking and engage with your spirit understanding to engage the realms of Heaven for the download of this information."

We prayed, *"I engage the realms of Heaven and ask angels to come to receive this revelation and assist me in every way in Jesus' name."*

Lucas explained, "A discussion of veils includes a discussion or an understanding of spheres. Let us start with the most common veil known to man—that veil written in scripture. In the temple of God, the veil was torn from the top to the bottom. It was completely torn apart by the power released to the earth through the body of Jesus, given in payment, that sons and daughters of God may know Him. The Heavens welcomed the removal of the veil in that hour, which had been foretold by prophets of the earth and by councils of Heavenly places, even the council among the Godhead. The tearing of the veil was a manifestation of His accomplishment of the mission for which He was sent—He came to remove the veil.

"Think of veils in large strokes with broader meaning. It is true that there remains now no enmity between God and man due to the veil removal. However, veils are still perceptible to mankind with your spirit being sensitive to veils of darkness that have been imposed upon the earth, put there by forces of darkness. But also veils, also called shields, which in this case are ones of protection, have been put in place by angels in the light, who hearken to or carry out the Word of the Lord.

"Jerusalem is described as the apple of the Lord's eye. Do you not have an eyelid that protects your own eye? It is a shield to your eye for what enters in that gate. Most often, the shield must come down to prevent unwanted intrusion through that gate. Therefore, just as your eyelid covers your eye, so a shield covers the apple of the Father's eye, which is the place of His rest, the place of His passion—Jerusalem. This shield is a created being of some classification."

Shields of Darkness

Lucas continued, "The shields that are erected by darkness are conjured using an occult pathway of darkness to achieve a similar effect. The saints of God have power over these illegal shields due to the occult shields' power coming illegally. According to the Justice of Heaven, decrees of the nature you are involved in regarding the pulling down of shields of an occult variety is important in this hour and is part of the work of your hands. By that, I mean the work of your mouth. Darkness has to have a shield covering it, otherwise the light of the world would penetrate the light of His Glory through His sons and daughters."

We asked, "How do people who are deceived into operating in league with darkness maintain their darkness?"

He replied, "By a shield, a conjured veil whose effect is to confuse, blur the lines, and distort vision so that workers of darkness can carry out secret deeds in darkness. But the light of the Lord who dwells in you richly is greater than their darkness. As sons and daughters of God, the release of light needs to go in tandem with the pulling down of veils—the pulling down of the covering that darkness is hiding under.

"When the saints agree with the work of Heaven that the timing is right for the pulling down of shields, in their dawning realization of their capacity to release angels who bring these shields down, their agreed faith, their decree, and the work of their mouth instructs the angelic realm in this destructive work. The removal of occult shields is a powerful tool to be used against those geographical places in the earth realm which occult darkness has put in place.

Shields Over Cities

"For example, there are certain cities that have these ungodly shields, these occult shields over them. One example in recent times is the city of Los Angeles which had an occult shield over it, but due to the work of the saints, the prayers of the saints, the decrees of the saints, and the boldness of the saints, the shield began to lose power. It began to be very weak and then there came a moment where angelic forces were released, and the shield was removed. Now the light can penetrate into LA in new ways." Lucas said, "This came to Donna's ears through Doug Addison. This is what she was hearing him talk about. On the day LA had a terrific electrical storm, that was that day that the shield was removed.

"You have heard of intense battles in the heavenlies by angels. This is true, and, if you could see it, it would look like the battle of sound wave frequencies. This is because often what is holding an occult shield in place is lack of worship from the saints, but where the King is worshiped, worship rises to begin to influence the occult shield. Know that the release of the sound of praise and worship with those who are releasing faith, love, honor, respect, acknowledgement, and the pure praises of God and of the King Jesus weaken the shields that are in place. This has happened in Washington, DC.[43]

"Following those among you who operate as generals and commanders on earth—yes, I am speaking of the apostolic sons and daughters of God—the body of Christ does well to engage a unified voice for the release of angels to reckon with these shields. Now is the time for the pulling down." He said, "Donna's understanding of the supernatural story over Jericho is true as you have described that."

"You are wondering how shields get established?" Lucas asked us, before answering for us, "This happens via works of darkness, the intent and will to engage with evil—whether the human is deceived or deluded or is intentionally rebelling against God to gain power from darkness. These ritual engagements have something to do with putting these occult shields into place. They do have to maintain them, and they often become children of wrath in the recognition of the ever looming need to keep these shields in place.

Shields Are Beings

"This is in contrast however, to the shields of Heaven that are being placed in dimensional places, not just geographical earth realm places by Yahweh. These shields that you refer to as beings are exactly that, and

---

[43] The time of this engagement was January 2021.

they have their own classification. These shields have a life form. They are in place on the pillars of the foundation of the earth."

Shields Are Objects

Lucas continued, "However, shields are also objects. They are heavenly in dimension and are built by the forces of angels. The work of worship, praise, proclaiming truth—just the simple proclaiming of truth—helps the angels establish the shield. Thus, homes of believing saints can have shields—that was Donna's vision—and evil cannot penetrate that. People can have these godly shields, groups can have these shields, places can have them—earthbound places—even gatherings can have them.

"Ask of the Father, 'Let the shields of the Lord be put in place.' This is an excellent prayer and decree of the saints. As the saints gather to pray for shields to be established, the shields themselves have innate understanding of their boundary. These are the shields of the Lord. They know their boundary."

He asked, "Which is greater? The shields of the Lord or the shields of the darkness? You know the light conquers all and has done so since eternal times when they were first established. Therefore, you can look at shields as a light wave being and its formation of light frequency resonates with the breath of God in the children of God—His sons and daughters. Therefore, their praise, their expression of truth, their verbal release of righteousness, their verbal release of the precepts of the Lord, and their verbal release of kindness, are frequencies and tones that agree with the working of the Heavenly shields.

"Remember what I told you? Occult shields distort vision. If you will look for it, you will see this in your day.

"It is where you second guess what you thought you saw, wondering if this is true or not. If it clouds your understanding, chances are you are trying to discern by looking with your natural eyes through an occult shield, when you must have discernment from your spirit man, because your spirit man, in conjunction with the discernment of the Lord by Holy Spirit, can discern through and penetrate through these shields. Therefore, the occult shields work so easily against the saints when they are not utilizing their spirit realm, their spirit eyes, and their spirit senses to discern with the power of the Spirit of God, His voice, the winds of God, and the messengers to decipher what is being seen. Therefore, saints often have a hunch that something is not as it should be. These hunches need to be paid attention to because you are beginning to understand the heavenly messengers of God, the voice of Holy Spirit, the discerning of spirits and truth, to reveal what is trying to be hidden from your sight by works of darkness. These hunches concern these occult shields that we have been talking about.

"Your discernment being liquid like a soap bubble is correct. Think about a soap bubble. In the physical earth, it is a manifestation of surface tension between the water and the soap. It is held together by the linking of those atoms or molecules. This is somewhat similar. The heavenly shields that can be placed by saints—it is a type of liquid forming the shield."

Donna interjected, "I have thought Lucas, that when you say it like that, you are meaning it is a formation of Holy Spirit, which seems to be liquid, which is a metaphor or a euphemism for the liquid protection."

Lucas replied, "Its consistencies operate in what you would call liquid."

Shields of Light

Lucas noted, "Light always overcomes darkness."

"Lucas, should I call them Shields of Light?" Donna asked.

He replied, "Yes, when you are requesting them. Notice I said requesting—we are not necessarily decreeing here."

"When we are talking about placing a shield, do we need Heaven's input on it?" we asked.

"Yes and no, because sometimes Shields of Light are placed because the saints get together to worship—they have gathered to seek the Kingdom, they have gathered to prophesy, they have gathered to be the conduit through which Heaven is expressed among themselves and the angels are building that."

Agreeing Voices

We asked, "So, when the occult shields of the earth are being torn down, the saints would decree this in agreement with Heaven. Is that right?"

Lucas replied, "An assault by light upon shields of darkness comes through the magnification of the agreeing voices of the children of God. These voices must stand in faith, trust, belief, and a firm stance. They must take hold of the grace of God for this. They must take hold of that while their spirit finds its flow of agreement. The natural senses will not assist in this. One must be okay with using the spirit senses to engage the decree that the bringing down of occult shields occurs at the hands of the angels assigned to bring them down."

"Ancient pagans knew about these shields. They did not know how they operated or what they had become engaged with, but they recognized a greater shield when they saw it. This is the story of the child, Moses, in the basket on the river. The basket represented the shield in which the baby lay. The pagan princess somehow recognized that was what that was at that time—a greater shield. The supernatural was a greater part of their day. Their intellect scientifically did not leap forward to make explanations, but her darkened senses of the invisible world gave her pause to consider this child who was not swamped but protected," Lucas explained.

"Lucas," we asked, "Is there anything else?"

Foul Birds

He began pointing out the connection between a shield erected or built by angels and the inability of foul birds[44] to penetrate. He was just reiterating that as it related to a recent vision Donna had where she was in her sunroom and suddenly a large pterodactyl-like creature flew into the glass of the enclosure. It was unable to penetrate the glass and Donna was protected from this evil intruder.

Replacing Occult Shields

We asked, "As an occult shield is dismantled, how is the godly shield put in place replacing the occult shield?"

Lucas replied, "As angels dismantle an occult shield, the shield of the righteous needs to fill the void. This is done by the expression of thanksgiving, the expression of joint unified voices expressing the power of God, the overwhelming victory of the King, the superior force of light, and the manifest expression of that, through their words—their conversation—they acknowledge the battle has been won. They testify. They release their

---

[44] Foul birds are discussed in later in Chapter 22.

witness and their agreement of the triumph of the Lord of Hosts through angel armies. This is the spark. This is what the angels then use to build the sphere, the godly sphere of protection that would fill that place. It is hard to imagine it, but it is a war of the spheres. Which one will fall? Which one will remain? Which one will overcome the other? Which one will force out the other? Think of it dimensionally like a soap bubble—not within a soap bubble, but one bubble vying for the same space as the other soap bubble. The greater kingdom power wins. This must be decreed by the saints as they are residents of the earth realm. 'Let the high praises of God be upon your lips' (Psalm 149). Does not the scripture say that? This is for the purpose of maintaining the placement these shields at the hands of the angels of God and preventing the activity of darkness from using the delusions and distrust of men."

The Football Stadium

Lucas then gave an example. "Think of the football arenas that you have been to. You go for fellowship, enjoyment, and activity. You go innocently. You go only with good thoughts, but you have entered under a sphere that you know not. Here is how I can tell you this, Donna."

He explained, "Do you remember that day you thought, 'Why is it so hard to have a thought about Jesus in this place?' That is due to the shield that is over that arena. Think of the unrighteous activities that you are not engaged in, but others are. There is betting, there are spirits of anger, spirits of division."

He says, "You have often wondered why a simple game of moving the football can get so heated that it affects the entire stadium. Have you noticed where it does this to the unwitting, to the unknowing, and to the people who engage in it without understanding? Think of that. Where you entered an ungodly sphere, you were under its influence. It was harder to have a thought of the will of God, the purposes of His destiny for the people in that place while you are there."

He explained, "Look at marketplaces. Take Disney, for example. When you are under the shield of that place—one that is not entirely righteous but built with deception—you come under a space that makes it very hard to have thoughts of actual reality. Do you think this is done by happenstance? It is not. You have encountered a shield.

"Let me show you another place. Remember years ago, when giant shopping malls were popular? It was covered by a shield. I am not saying that everyone engaged in shopping was engaged in evil, but when you entered that place, there were forces of darkness trying to impact the behavior and activity of humans to manipulate and control what they thought about and what they said. That is occult shields. Do not be naive. Occult shields are put in place with intention. They use deceived and deluded humans—humans that are in league with darkness, whether due to bloodlines or whether due to trauma inflicted in their life that induces them to rebel against God. People have created a shield of darkness over those places so that you are manipulated when you get there. Some of this is just the activity of evil prayer. It is the working of darkness.

"Those who hear you speak of this will be prone to this that I am about to describe. There is a pendulum swing that people are going to go through where they see 'everything is a shield'. And then it will swing back the other way, where their thoughts will be, 'Nothing is a shield.' This is complete stupidity. Eventually, that pendulum of new truth that you release will land in the middle and Holy Spirit will bring about a balance in His people. Where you do not see the balance in someone's grasp of this is where they have not consulted with Holy Spirit to let Him teach them about this revelation. Nevertheless, is it right to hold light under a barrel?" Lucas concluded.

. . . . .

One reason for the inclusion of this information in this book is that the Body of Christ needs to be requesting Shields of Light over our homes, businesses, churches, ministries, families, schools, government, and more. Because of our ignorance, much darkness has been allowed to reign. Hidden things of darkness need to be uncovered. Where trading floors have been impacted by occult shields, those shields need to come down and Shields of Light replace them. Proverbs 29:2 declares:

> *When the righteous are in authority, the people rejoice: but when the wicked rule, the people mourn.*

Your political party does not have to be the dominant party for the Body of Christ to rule as the ecclesia in the spirit arena. Righteous rulership, regardless of who is in office, is essential for the overall well-being of the nations of the earth. Let us beseech the Lord for the Shields of Light to be placed throughout the earth.

Chapter 17
Realms & Dimensions

We started this engagement with Mitchell. A question had arisen about something he briefly mentioned the prior week, where he taught us about 12 heavens and 33 dimensions. For clarity, I asked if realms were within dimensions. His instruction is summarized in this chapter.

Mitchell began, "You can think of the 12 heavens as vertical, from earth up. The 33 dimensions are classifications of other containers that hold varieties of realms. Earth is one realm. In a progression, you can gain access through the 12 heavens.

"Of the 33 dimensions, each dimension can contain realms. The realms travel from dimension to dimension, while at the same time, that dimension gains increased access to higher realms and higher heavens," he explained.

To grasp this better, we asked for an example of how earth is a dimension that contains realms.

He explained, "Just think of all the entities that exist. There are saints who are physically bound, but in the spirit, each has a realm and is inside a dimension. However, do not think of a dimension as a natural plane. You need a different understanding of it because it feels quantum and in time, and it feels stacked, layered, or encircled at the same time. Then, as these dimensions expand through trade (that is where the trade routes come in), the Kingdom of God (which is in the 12 heavens) expands too. You and your dimension can expand or grow. As it does, the realms inside that dimension have greater knowledge, understanding, access, and power, which comes from the levels of the heavens."

Further clarifying, Mitchell said, "Something about the realms inside the dimension helps it to grow and fill its destiny scroll. As the dimension grows, those inside of it expand with their realms. Not everyone has to do that at the same time though, because a remnant is always present. There are always forerunners and pioneers. As they grow, it affects the dimension so that the realms inside of it get an automatic increase because it always takes somebody to go first."

He continued, "This is also connected to trade, as the realms inside the dimension trade in other dimensions and other realms. This has been going on for a while, but we were unaware and unfortunately, it has mostly been co-opted by darkness. Humans and their realms have engaged illegally in trade. This means that things which are not the will of the Father for certain things in other dimensions and the realms within those dimensions have occurred."

Light or Dark

He expounded, "Each dimension has both light and darkness. It is the plan of the Father for every dimension to become more light-filled (like on earth). This occurs through the saints and their expression of the Kingdom, or the level of the heavens they have been granted."

Concluding, he said, "The pleasure of the Father (and all the other realms know this) is that because His Glory presence manifested in the form of Jesus in the earth realm, this dimension is marked for preeminence. This means that someday it will reflect the fullness of the glory of all 12 heavens and its dimension will be changed. The heavens will be rolled back like an old garment, and all other dimensions and their realms will trade with this new earth dimension and its realms, because this is the way the Father planned it. This is how Jesus will receive all glory from every realm in every dimension. This is how the saints will steward the other dimensions, trading with all dimensions in that day."

Chapter 18
Understanding Realms

Our instructor for this encounter with Heaven was Malcolm. He wanted to give us an understanding of realms. He began, "Realms of Heaven are what you would call galactic or intergalactic. They are represented by spheres. Your spirit and your star are like this. The planet is like this, and the realms of Heaven can flow in and out of these spherical containers. They are many and varied. They each contain a flavor of the expression of God's knowledge, wisdom, power, and might. The Father and the Son, through the power of Holy Spirit, know all things in all realms from cycle to cycle. To understand this, you will need to consider the density of time. You will need to think of time as dense layers of cycles."

Malcolm continued, "Imagine taking a slinky and putting its ends together, and what do you have? You have a spherical donut-shaped object with layers, each ring representing a layer. Now, imagine those rings are without end. Realize that realms are related to time, but it is easier to say that they are linked to time density. Some realms have yet to be opened, as they are reserved for other cycles. Some realms have been closed, having completed their revolution."

Building Realms

He went on to explain, "When you open the silver channel,[45] you are opening a passage to a realm. When you build from creativity, you are building a realm, because you are made like the Father and you are an heir. Those made like the Father who are not heirs build realms of darkness in league with total darkness. They capture things in those realms and therefore Satan needs them and is using them. He has convinced them through deception, but he holds them in bondage, some having given themselves over to him. Their realm has become not only dark, but a hollow, vast wasteland of nothing. This causes them to seek to deceive others, so that that they might capture another's realm."

He added, "This capturing of realms is what you see in satanic rituals. They use the soul, or the 3-D plane, to access the realm within the person. Therefore, they intentionally fragment soul realms. They are seeking after the spirit realm that is connected to the soul realm."

---

[45] Opening the Silver Channel refers to one of the steps for releasing lingering human spirits. See *Lingering Human Spirits* by Dr. Ron M. Horner.

Malcolm elaborated, "To you, your realm is protected with the blood of Jesus and with angelic activity. It is protected with the Word of God and with righteous deeds. It is protected by a position that seeks to be filled by Holy Spirit, so that the clash of these realms in the density of time takes place.

"There are many realms in your Father's Kingdom. Not all realms are available to you as natural, living beings. However, your spirit will eternally investigate realms, creating within the Father's massive realm His expression through you and through your spirit. Nations are also realms, having been built by a collective agreement."

Levels of Agreement Create Realms

Malcolm continued this fascinating teaching, "Do you see how levels of agreement create levels of realms? A neighborhood is a realm. A city is a realm. When two or more individuals agree, a realm is created—the individuals are filled with the agreement. This is what happened to Eve. She gave agreement to the one who coveted the realm she was responsible for stewarding. She had assignment to multiply. She came out of agreement with Adam and into agreement with darkness. This was a trade, and when other realms saw a human trade like this, it created illegal trading floors where they wondered at the centrality of Almighty God. A portion of these other realms saw that they could trade with the offspring of Yahweh in illegal ways. This still goes on today. These illegal trading floors will be overthrown, and this is happening even now."

Steward Your Realm

"As you can see, you must steward your realm," he instructed. "As you steward your realm with what you call the ways of Yahweh, you enlarge and empower it, and it becomes recognized by other realms. As you think larger, you began to see an unlocking effect. Some realms only desire to trade with human realms that are filled with light because that realm is associated with the Most High. They are convinced of His centrality, meaning His Word is truth. He is who He is, as He told Moses. The statement, "I am that I am," was a signal to other realms, but it so filled Moses' realm with ability that he was able to accomplish what he did."

Concluding he said, "Many realms are watching this play out. Innumerable realms exist that you want to and can trade with. What they trade from is an expression in their realm of who the Father is. Those who are lacking the Father's light and the centrality of who He is—they trade from deception, control, bondage, and plunder. They trade what they have stolen from other realms because they have nothing good to trade. Right now, they are trading for your words. For this reason, you must speak the Word of God in season and out of season. Realms desire to trade off the words of the heirs of Yahweh."

Chapter 19

Location, Location, Location

As we engaged Heaven for more revelation, Lydia opened with "I want to talk about location, location, location." You have likely heard this phrase regarding establishing business or offices, but Heaven had more in mind that just bricks, sticks, and stuff. Lydia continued speaking, "Your understanding of geography, and dimensional access, and the realms of Heaven has been growing. You have been increasing in the awareness and the knowledge of powers and principalities. You have become aware of systems, realms of darkness, dimensional places - such as under the earth, under the water, above the earth, you have learned about bridges, the routes that angels take, and you have also been learning about how angels circumvent the enemy, taking his lead away from him, preventing him access, plundering his camp, and gaining back what he has taken.

"Location is a key to defeating the usurper. Your placement and position in Christ Jesus labels you with an authority that has already defeated any darkness. Every level of darkness is a step down from the light that you not only carry, but the light you have access to, and the light that dwells in you."

Your knowledge and understanding of your location in Jesus and His location in you is a key to understanding oneness.

She continued, "It is a key to understanding governmental rule from the kingdom of God. It is the key to recognition of the release of his power and the beloved status of humankind by the Father. Also revealed is His desire to indwell you as human with Himself - not only by His spirit, but by giving you a place in the first. Remember Jesus was the first and the Father has placed you inside the first and as human realizes their positioning, they will increasingly cast out darkness working with angels to prevent its entry. Learn to fine tune the light so they may direct it against the works of darkness so that every evil thing is exposed and becomes governed by the righteous King.

"Your understanding of your location is what Paul was saying about your position in Christ and your location center is being synchronized, shifted, and realized. Ponder your location as a spiritual being *in* a spiritual being and take possession of that realm fully as you link arms metaphorically with others in the Bride of Christ. To link arms with you increases the expansion of the position of the Bride as a whole and brings the nuances and layers of the Kingdom of God to more evidence in the physical plane and in the natural realm than ever before.

“As the saints began to recognize their spiritual position, their spiritual location, their access, and their invitation to explore the realms of their location they will begin to understand that this is the invitation of the hour and to many it clashes with their soul as their spirit begins to real realize how limited the soul has kept the spirit. As the spirit is cleansed, the soul is cleansed, and the spirit becomes more positioned within the being of that individual.

“I am telling you a mystery and I am assisting in the explanation of a paradigm of the dawning of the recognition of your location which is central to the reflection of His glory into the realm of earth. These things make devils tremble—many devils tremble and flee before you when you operate with the look of knowledge of the location of your position. Many have understood the throne and have understood the King who sits upon the throne and yet there is a gulf of understanding of your location and His rule—His absolute rule over all that is just now dawning on the sons and daughters of Yahweh. This will bring forth changes into the physical plane that the creation of the physical plane has longed for, looked for, and expected.

“The creation itself (by that I mean the physical creation) has memory of the promise of its freedom from corruption, darkness, misalignment, and unrighteousness. Even the creation pulls upon the grace of the Father, through His sons and daughters who know their location in Him, and the portals are releasing His glory into the earth realm.

"What I could tell you about how this is going to play out would shock you, but I'm going to refrain from detail because the reasoning behind my releasing of this to you is for your own pondering."

Jerusalem

At this point, Lydia had Donna look at Jerusalem and was saying to Donna, "Jerusalem is a clock." Donna was not seeing Jerusalem like the geography of the place—the physical place. Rather, she was seeing it like a sphere of movement like the movements of a clock.

Lydia noted, "Remember, location is important."

Chapter 20
Disruptors

Mitchell had a new subject in mind: the understanding of a disruptor. He began, "Many things are set against the Kingdom of God as the long-term war between light and darkness plays out in yet another battle skirmish. Our enemy, Satan, is designing disruptors. These are meant to shock, surprise, paralyze, and wreak havoc in the flow of times and seasons. These disruptors planned by the enemy are always known beforehand by the Father, and He warns the Bride of Christ through signs, words, dreams, and knowings to His children.

What we have been experiencing with the pandemic caused by COVID-19 has come from the release of a disruptor. The world will recover from this, yet some will be so infected by fear that, like the generation that died in the wilderness, they will not overcome that fear. They will go to their grave with it, having been disrupted by this trauma. When human beings have not accessed Heaven to be healed, through their choice or deceptive agreement with fear, they may remain in that state until death. It is not that the Father could not heal them, but they must access the healing.

However, the Father does have tools, decrees, and righteous ones, which are holy beings sitting on councils in Heaven who work to circumvent the enemy in his plans of disruption, to the point of victory. This will require the saints to draw close to the Lord Jesus, the King, so they can hear what they are to do."

Regional & Geographic Disruptors

He continued, "Note that disruptors are often regional and geographical. These regions suffer because of heavenly warfare, where the angels of the host of Heaven are engaged in intense, very literal war against the usurper and his evil ones.

"In some cases, these evil ones are humans. They have made alignment with darkness and trade with the enemy, and he uses them wickedly. They do not really know what they have committed to trade with. George Soros is one of these.

"However, the Father is never outdone by the workings of the enemy. The Father has plans for the saints regarding the disruptor and the disruptions.

The glory of God is a being,
a weapon, and an entity.

“The enemy knows that the expansion of glory through the children of God and their realms, as He fills their realms with glory, is more powerful than the saints realize. The enemy trembles to know he has no weapon against this. He fears that the saints will come to understand how to utilize glory, as well as how it operates in the earth through them, on them, in them, and with them to defeat him.

“Weapons of Glory are stored in a warehouse in the Heavens and laid in great piles. They are living beings in the form of light. You could almost say they are orbs of energy,” he explained.

A Coming Disruptor

Warning us, Mitchell stated, “A coming disruptor in the nation of the saints is an attack of paralysis, which will paralyze the voice and movement, and cause hopelessness through a lack of vision. It will come on the heels of the COVID disruption. This disruptor is meant to cause shock. I tell you now that this has already been overcome so that do you not fall into the pit of paralysis. Know that you will cross over to the other side, and you will be protected by God and His realm. You will be protected by His name. You will be protected by His glory, as His glory will manifest.

The operation of the saints is to agree with Glory, to take possession of it in their realm, and to release the Glory through their words, deeds, and even prophetic acts in this hour. This is because the saints have more access to it now, and in future days, the Father will release more of it because of the destruction which is being planned by the enemy. The Glory released defeats the enemy's plans.

You will need to stay close to what Heaven is saying and what you hear from apostles and prophets. Remain steadfast and immovable in your stance and attitude toward the disruption. The disruption coming will not be like the corona virus. It may be like it in effect, but it will be different in its release. Once it has come, one day you will realize, "Oh, this is what Mitchell was talking about."

Nevertheless, businesses in the kingdom realm are preserved. The continued work of our ministry is to release this word to those who come near who have business interests.

Our encouragement to the saints to hear and see will continue. The network that is being developed and strengthened from Ezekiel's activity even now will need to be stewarded when it happens. There is more to tell, but you cannot bear it just now."

Going further Mitchell said, "Remember what I told you. You have enough information to know that you must continue to press on. Keep your eyes focused on Heaven and keep going because this will pass. This cannot possibly win.

Mitchell told us that with assurance and informed us that we will be in this for a little while longer. The Father has preserved for Himself a remnant who are marching on encampments of the enemy and making incredible headway in our day. It falls to the generals to know what to do and where to release ranks. Your Father has many generals at work.

In this disruption, do not hunker down to ride it out. Instead, **increase the hidden activity of worship and praise**. Receive the hidden joy, which is like manna from heaven. Eat of this hidden manna of joy and you will be strengthened to continue."

He continued, "Heaven is serious, but not worried or anxious. Heaven is simply letting you know. You must trust God in this. You must trust what you know from our realm and that it is enough.

Remember that revelation always flows to the children of God who are seeking for it. Where there is a greater need for the revelation to flow, a wider flow will occur. Be encouraged to receive revelation from the hand of the Father. He has things to say to you, often daily, to help you be victorious. This is the access given to you by the King Jesus himself. He will not fail. He cannot fail because He has already won.

Heaven is releasing a mindset to be able to understand this and walk with it. Receive it and prophetically place it in your own mind as taking hold of the mind of Christ.

If you know what is happening, then you can operate in the opposite spirit. Arm yourself with the knowledge of God's grace that you have access to, so you are prepared. When you know what you are dealing with, it is easier to get through it."

Anyone can receive daily revelation from the Father so you know what to expect and can prepare for it. This is the purpose of hearing from your Father, so you know what to do. This is a grace which comes in your hour of need if you are paying attention. God's mercy can get it to us, but we do need to turn our faces and hearts to Him. We must pause to say, "I do not know at all, but you have a great plan. What is the next step?"

Heaven is giving us a heads up.

Chapter 21
Disrupting the Disruptor

The weather was extremely windy and unsettled outside as we engaged Heaven one Thursday. It seemed representative of the turmoil in the heavenlies. We were scheduled with a meeting with Ezekiel who appeared with an hourglass in his hand. He had something he wanted to show us that was completely new so, he began to explain what the hourglass represented. What he was holding was a timed explosive device. Satan has his version of this device which is always meant for destruction while the Father has his version which is meant for destruction of the realms of darkness and expansion of the Kingdom of God. I will not in this letter give all the details, but simply provide you a little of the backstory.

The enemy has multiple plan disruptions over the next short while and as the ecclesia we need to be aware and be ready to release Heaven's weaponry for those events in advance of them.

Ezekiel began to explain, "A planned disruption is known to the King and He desires the sons of His Kingdom to plant his own timed devices against forces of darkness and evil. This evil is not humankind being led astray or deceived. This is spiritual forces of darkness, principalities, and thrones set against the Kingdom of God in direct opposition against the Godhead who have led many astray and whom some worship. The evil is evil. This evil is worse than you think it is. It is deep darkness, deep evil, the destroyer along with the wicked variety of kingdoms—underwater and celestial—other races. Their planned destruction has been timed as a disruption and it is now time for the sons of God to release the timing devices of Yahweh, of the Kingdom of Glory into the world.

"In response to the enemy's planned disruption, the Father is releasing His own disruptors, His own timing devices. This timing device is a Kingdom Glory. This is a good thing. These timing devices are not for destruction. They are for the building up of the church and they are released as a response like the Father dares the enemy to use his disruptor because the Father then comes in with His overwhelming power of goodness and grace and causes moves of God, movements of the church, awakenings, even miracles, and things of that sort. We can count on this victory as we join the Lord in the air to release His timing devices—His own weapons of timed devices. We can do this with joy because it overwhelms darkness with light.

"Angels are amassed and ready to release the Father's timed devices into the earth and the dark spiritual regions but is awaiting the participation of the saints. The ecclesia (which is 2 or more saints in agreement) must arise and release prayers in this regard.

"Two ways exist to release this:

1) Simply an agreed upon prayer between two saints touching in agreement that time devices would be planted with the activity of undercover angels (stealth mode) and that they would plant these according to the maps of Heaven.

2) Where saints agree that the time device of the Lord would be catapulted into dark regions. Dark regions are not global. Dark regions are spiritual. It is not a physical place. It is spiritual. Dark regions are spiritual regions of darkness. Saints can agree that angels will catapult these time devices of the Lord into them for their effect within the time of the season and the era for which they were created."

He continued, "This weapon is not something that is available to us always. It is released only at certain times. There is a timing element of when it is available. It is only available at certain times and angels know when it is available, and they can let you know when it is available. Therefore, we were informed this day by Ezekiel (our ministry's angel).

"It is not unlimited. It is for a time. It is like a time within a time. So, there is a moment in time where angels know this weapon is released to be used by the saints. It is not inexhaustible. It has a supply and when the supply is over it is over. The church and members of the Bride (the praying ecclesia which is all saints agreeing as touching this thing), are to release the angels to do their work in prayer by faith. This is a very specialized, highly regarded weapon of the Lord."

"Is one method preferred over the other?" we asked.

Ezekiel replied, "Both are needed. Some will have more faith for one than the other. They will have more understanding of one than the other. Pray the prayer that you can pray with the most faith."

Heaven even gave us the prayer to pray:

Prayer for Timed Devices of the King of Glory for Distribution by the Hands of Angels Requested by the Saints in Prayer

Prayer 1:

In the name of the King, in agreement with scripture that says where two or more are gathered in the name of the King of glory, we choose now to co-labor with Heaven from earth regarding...

The Request of the Release of Timed Devices *of the King of Glory to be released into the earth; to be stealthily placed at the hands of angels of the* *heavenly host for this purpose; that Yahweh succeeds to victory and overwhelms the enemy due to the timed devices deployment and their intended effect and results.*

We praise the Lord for his magnificent power, ability, and magnanimous virtue to overcome darkness, to turn evil to good, and to arrange His splendor upon the face of the earth.

We agree with this work and the release of the angels of the host of Heaven, all associated angels engaged with this assignment to their work, commissioning them as the Sons of God in the name of Jesus Christ.

Prayer 2:

To Deploy Time Devices to the Realms of Darkness:

In the name of the King, in agreement with scripture that says where two or more are gathered in the name of the King of glory, we choose now to co-labor with Heaven from earth regarding...

The Request of the Release of Timed Devices to be Catapulted into Regions of Darkness. *We agree with the work of the Father, His love of the saints, His love for Jesus, His love for Himself, so as the three parts of the Trinity love* *themselves, we agree with this for the work of kindness, to the work of goodness, for the result of their agreement in cosmic geographies that affect planet earth. We come into agreement with His rule and reign in all spaces and release the angels of the host to their work regarding the release of the catapult containing time devices of the Glory of God.*

We praise the Lord for his magnificent power, ability, and magnanimous virtue to overcome darkness, to turn evil to good, and to arrange His splendor upon the face of the earth.

We agree with this work and the release of the angels of the host of Heaven, all associated angels engaged with this assignment to their work, commissioning them as the Sons of God in the name of Jesus Christ.

Thank you for co-laboring with Heaven and joining us in verbally releasing angels to do this work for the Kingdom and for the nations of the earth.

Chapter 22

The Foul Birds of Revelation 18:2

Sometimes we must adjust to receive insights that are outside of our understanding. The following chapter is on a subject that the Body of Christ needs to understand. To receive this information, our souls and spirits must be prepared for it. Heaven told us, "The following are some instructions to help prepare you to receive this information:

- Pray in tongues first—take a moment to pray in tongues.
- Call your spirit forward to receive.
- Renounce fear at every level—do this aloud, not silently.
- Ask Holy Spirit to broaden your mind so you can capture this information.
- Remind them that they signed up for this when they engaged their desire to mature and that the Lord knows every heart.

"When you pray in tongues," Heaven clarified, "you are building a structure for revelation to abide in." Praying in tongues builds our faith and enlarges our capacity to receive revelation of a spiritual nature. Take a few moments to pray in the spirit, aloud if possible. Pray until you are in a place where you are ready to receive revelation.

Secondly, call your spirit forward to receive this revelation. As we have talked about in other parts of this book, our souls are not qualified or equipped to receive revelation. Revelation must come first to our spirits before it can be translated to our souls.[46]

Our third instruction involved renouncing any fear that we may have in our lives on any level. Satan knows he can paralyze us with fear. When you know whose you are and who you are, you understand that there is no reason to fear anything or anyone. Where you have the presence of fear demonstrates a place where the love of God is missing in that arena. John 4:18 says:

> *Fear cannot co-exist in this love realm (where the love of the Father is embraced). The perfect love union that we are talking about expels fear. Fear holds on to an expectation of crisis and judgment. It echoes torment and only registers in someone who does not yet realize the completeness of their love union. (THE MIRROR) (Emphasis mine)*

---

[46] Read "Learning to Live Spirit First" in the Appendix for more information on this subject.

Where we have embraced fear, we need to repent, renounce it, and allow Holy Spirit to fill that place with the Father's love.[47] Let us take a moment, search our hearts, and renounce any fear.

> *Father, I come to repent for embracing fear on any level in my life. Where I have embraced fear or where I have allowed fear to dominate any area of my life, I repent. I only want you to dominate my life. I want your love to conquer me.*
>
> *I ask your forgiveness, in Jesus' name, and I ask that you fill every place where fear has existed with your power, security, peace, and love, in Jesus' name.*
>
> *I choose to come out of agreement with fear NOW, in Jesus' name. Let your love conquer me now, I ask, in Jesus' name.*

Our fourth instruction was to ask Holy Spirit for capturing abilities of broadness of mind. To make it simpler, ask Holy Spirit to broaden your mind so you can capture this information. Let us ask Holy Spirit to broaden us to receive what Heaven is sharing.

Finally, Heaven pointed out that you basically signed up for this. You may have been intrigued by the title of the book, or the title of this chapter, or you may simply be hungry for revelation, but regardless of the reason, you are here. Step in now, with boldness, and receive.

---

[47] Read Psalm 23 in The Passion Translation.

. . . .

Revelation 18:2

It was early spring when Donna and I approached the Help Desk in the Business Complex of Heaven on this occasion. "We would like someone who could instruct us on Revelation 18:2," we inquired. I had written a book on lingering human spirits[48] and this verse held a clue to something that was unexplained elsewhere in the scriptures. I determined the best place to find out what I needed to know was from Heaven itself. Heaven has tutors that can assist us in an infinite variety of areas, and this was no different.

The verse reads:

> *And he cried mightily with a loud voice, saying, "Babylon the great is fallen, is fallen, and has become a dwelling place of demons, a prison for every foul spirit, and a cage for every* ***unclean and hated bird****! (Revelation 18:2) (Emphasis mine)*

Within moments of making our request for a tutor we found ourselves at the general Help Desk in the realms of Heaven rather than the Help Desk in the Business Complex. Again, we repeated our request. "We request a tutor or someone who can give us revelation about

---

[48] *Lingering Human Spirits* by Dr. Ron M. Horner (LifeSpring Publishing, 2020).

Revelation 18:2, specifically regarding the terms that were used about the unclean spirits, the demons, and the unclean birds."

We were introduced to a tutor named James, one of the men in white linen whom we followed to a classroom.

"We are interested in knowing the meaning of Revelation 18:2, with specific interest in the definitions behind the words: demons, unclean spirit, unclean and hateful bird," we explained. Thus, our instruction began.

James explained, "The key is in noticing the location of each: the demons dwell there, unclean spirits are imprisoned, and the unclean and hateful birds are in prison (or caged) there as well." He said, "I can instruct you if you are willing to learn."

At that moment, we set down all preconceived notions to learn what Heaven had to share.

James began, "Babylon here is a realm. The demons are demonic entities fallen from Heaven and their procreated offspring. The unclean spirits would be the spirits of mankind—spirits of man imprisoned in this place.[49] The hateful birds, the unclean birds, are messengers of evil, having assignments against humanity. Their nature is foreign to the earth's realm. They feed upon the ritualistic abuse that humanity

---

[49] See my book, *Lingering Human Spirits* (2020) LifeSpring Publishing.

engages in. You would call that profane worship. They are imprisoned in that realm until their appointed times to be released from that realm for their wicked assignments on the earth by the rulers of that realm who are the principalities of evil."

A Hybrid Creation

He continued, "The unclean birds of the air refer to spiritual entities that are the devices of evil realms sent out on missions and assignments against the humanity God has created. Their form is ungodly, wicked, and evil. They create havoc upon the earth. They are reserved for evil times, although their procreation is what is being developed by laboratories under the direction of evil men. You would call them hybrids. Their procreation is by unnatural means and is not what humans engage in. They are used as tools to wreak havoc, bring ruination and disturbance, and even bring many humans into temptation.

The assignments of foul birds are more focused than demons and are extremely specific.

"They are often released as a horde against a population when evil has knowledge that they are either ready or have been prepared for this evil attack.

"These foul birds are little known by the church and lesser known by unbelievers.

They originate from realms or dimensions of evil out of timelines of darkness.

"They are extremely focused on their assignment and it seems they have a time and a season. They are created for the purpose of a specific time release within seasons. Where you and I might call that time and date, that realm operates more on ages, seasons, and eras. A lot of this is held in reserve for future days but not all.

"Their making is wicked and revolting, and thus the term unclean. Their hybrid status is outside the realm of divine will and goes totally against the estate in which their creators themselves were formed. Their creation was formed by darkness alone, often using technologies in devious manners for this purpose and their sustenance. These creatures are a mixture of the natural realm and spiritual realms. They are infused with spiritual power from darkness, and their increased presence on planet earth is through portals of darkness. Some humans have put themselves in league with darkness to bring these entities demonstratively into the earth, against permitted timelines.

"These are wicked birds of the air. They come to steal the Word of God from men's hearts. This is like the parable of the sower Jesus talked about.[50] These are unseen messengers of wickedness from realms of

[50] See Mark 4.

darkness, working with the intent of theft *and* to make men's hearts fail. John saw this in the Revelation.

We had a series of questions for James at this point.

"Was John seeing their greater influence in the future of earth?" we wondered.

"Yes," He replied.

We asked, "Have they been released into the earth before?"

"In measure, but never so bold as in these days," was his response.

"And how do we deal with them?"[51] we inquired.

James told us, "Angelic hosts have weapons against them. Here is one thing that is different about them. Because of their hybrid nature, they do not seek a host, so they do not seek to dwell in or near a person or a creature, like an animal. That is what will freak people out." You are accustomed to demons or spirits seeking a host but that is not so with these creatures.

He reminded us, "You know how you've been using the angels with the fluorescent paint to uncover workers of darkness?"[52] He continued, "Sometimes you are finding these creatures on assignment against people but quite often they seek to use stealth in their attacks. They

---

[51] More about this later in this chapter.

[52] In certain ministry sessions where demons or evil spirits were seeking to remain hidden, we request angels to paint them with fluorescent paint, so they are no longer hidden. Then we deal with them.

will stay hidden if possible. The more the sons of God utilize the angelic hosts for the capture and delivery in chains, of these creatures to Jesus, the more effective the sons of God will be in their authority and rule for the redemption of the earth."

What Class are They?

"Would you call these a class of demon?" we asked.

"They are not really a class of demons. They are a subset or category of their own. This is a worsening of the wrath of hell. They know no depth or limit of evil. They do not know the boundary of evil. They are always after evil and the pursuit of the intentionality of evil has played a part in their creation. Theirs is an expression of the depth of wickedness," he replied.

We wondered, "Have we, in our sessions with clients, come across them at times?"

"Yes, a few times. You often see them with people who have been ritualized. They will have an assigned bird of the air against them. This is because a lot of them are fractured and fragmented. These people generally have fragmented souls as well as fragmented spirits."

"They are birds because their assignment is to brood over you for evil. Think about how a mother bird in the natural earth broods over her young for good. Foul birds brood, but for evil purposes. The person—the human—is not *captured* by them but is *brooded over* by them. Their limiting presence is always felt, or they may limit the person's spiritual activity. An example of this might be where someone tries to engage their spirit with Holy Spirit or to reach out to the heavenly realms but is unsuccessful because of the brooding presence of this unclean bird, which is preventing it," he responded.

Dealing with the Birds

Our next question was, "How do we deal with these creatures?"

"Utilize the angelic force to release the nets of Heaven to capture these birds," he answered. "A fowler[53] is one who captures birds. Release the heavenly fowlers, the angels that operate in that method.

"The nets are frequencies that Heaven has intwined with the gold of Heaven like filaments. Any lesser net would not be effective."

Detecting the Foul Birds

"How can we detect that this is what we are dealing with?" we inquired.

"When in ministry sessions, you can look to see the birds, but you must *look* to see them. They can also be discovered by using angels to bring light to them to remove their cloaking and to reveal their hiding places."

---

[53] Psalm 91:3 Surely, He shall deliver you from the snare of the fowler and from the perilous pestilence.

"What would the wording for that be?" we asked.

> *"I request the angels of Heaven to bring the light of God's glory to light up every hidden and dark space in the realm of the person that I am ministering to. Light it up like daylight and startle the birds so that I can see them.*

"In most cases you will be able to see them. Then, call in angelic hosts. Call in the fowler to capture the bird, remembering to seek for repentance, if any is needed, if the person has made agreement to be brooded over. Often, they have made agreements unknowingly or in seasons of sleep," was his response.

Have They Made Agreements?

"Does that mean they were experiencing something like a trance, hypnosis, or fragmentation where this was perpetrated to get the persons agreement where they do not even know they gave agreement?" we asked.

"This often happens during ritualized torture. All agreement with the brooding action, or agreements to be brooded over by the foul birds, must be repented for, renounced, and covered by the Blood of the Lamb," James instructed. "This gains a measure of freedom and then angels can go to work. Do not be surprised if you are not able to see them right away. By practicing this, you will receive more focused help to do so. This is difficult to see or discern, but not impossible," he replied.

To detect them:

- Look to see the birds, but you must *look* to see them or use angels to bring light to them to remove their cloaking and to reveal their hiding places.

- Use this prayer:

  I request the angels of Heaven to bring the light of God's glory to light up every hidden and dark space in the realm of the person that I am ministering to. Light it up like daylight and startle the birds so that I can see them.

- All agreement with the brooding action, or agreements to be brooded over by the foul birds, must be repented for, renounced, and covered by the Blood of the Lamb.

- Utilize the angelic forces to release the nets of Heaven to capture these birds. A fowler[54] is one who captures birds.

- Release the heavenly fowlers, the angels that operate in that method.

(More instructions were given in a later engagement and will be detailed later in this chapter.)

---

[54] Psalm 91:3 Surely, He shall deliver you from the snare of the fowler and from the perilous pestilence.

Symptoms of Brooding

"What symptoms would a person feel of being brooded over like this?" we questioned.

James explained, *"They would feel a sense of limitation,* but not as though they are limited by lingering human spirits. It is not like you are carrying out someone else's burden. It is more of a sense of *not being able to press through to a level.*

"James showed us a picture of a natural, healthy mother bird in a nest beating back her young to keep them in the nest because she knows they are too young to attempt flight. By doing so, she manages to keep them in the nest until their strength has increased."

He explained, "This feeling of limitation is the opposite of that, in that they are buffeted back, and the person feels limited whenever they attempt spiritual activity and are never able to really get there."

He directed, "Do not look for this on lots of people. It is not generalized yet in the earth, but it is specific to people who have been ritualized.

Tied to Mithraism

"Believe it or not, this is tied to Mithraism's[55] first degree, the Corax (or the Raven) degree. Some

---

[55] For understanding of Mithraism, it's impact, and how to get free, see my book *Freedom from Mithraism.*

association exists in that it feels ancient. Somehow, a connection with Mithraism is involved."

"Is there anything else we have missed asking you?" we inquired, having learned from past experiences that asking this allows for further expansion of our knowledge, and Heaven likes when do so.

James replied, "Practice what you have learned and take note of what happens and what is felt. *Operate with confidence* against these creatures. A caution here is that knowledge of this nature to the unskilled or the immature puts them at risk. Since they have eaten from the wrong tree, the Tree of the Knowledge of Good and Evil, they will take that knowledge and they will try to operate in it. It is not for the immature. Therefore, in some regard, it is somewhat mysterious still."

With that, this engagement with James was over. We had plenty to ponder since this was not a topic that was taught in my Sunday School growing up. We were not released to share this information when we first received it in the spring of 2020, but we knew that we would be released to share it in the future.

. . . .

Months later, realizing there was more to be discovered on this topic in light of recent national events, Donna and I re-engaged Heaven. This time Mitchell was our instructor, and he brought out some of the same points as James, but also he unveiled some different insights. As you read, understand that the combined information from James and Mitchell gives us a much more comprehensive picture, as well as giving us steps to take to overcome and stop these foul creatures.

The Destruction They Bring

Mitchell began by pointing out the destruction a foul bird would bring. He began, "Foul birds are beings of destruction with a particular release of a sound frequency and wings for mounting the sky (or atmospheres). They engage in hovering, gliding, entering a realm from an overhead position, as in a bird's eye view, and they release resistant sound wave frequencies into the atmosphere. These frequencies have effects in the physical realm on all things related to frequencies whether sound, light, or radio waves, even Wi-Fi internet frequencies. They could even affect the weather. These foul birds shape sound frequencies with the purpose of disruption.

"Picture someone holding their hands over their ears to block out a piercing sound or visualize a dog that is immobilized because he hears a particular frequency. The dog is completely undone by the intensity of the frequency being generated. From the mouths (or beaks) of these birds is a type of screech. Think of the winged creatures in *The Lord of the Rings* movies. The screeches are for the destruction and devastation of something. They seek to destroy plans and purposes."

We were reminded that recently Ezekiel (our ministry angel) had been requesting shields. Mitchell began to explain how they function, “These shields act like a dome to protect what is inside of it, but it is not merely a covering over the top or sides of something. It is more spherical so that the coverage is on all sides—above, around, and underneath. We have seen these domes pictured in movies. Something called national shields exists as well as shields over cities and regions. Thrones are connected to shields. We say a thing is ruling in an area even if it is an unseen thing, it is connected to a throne.

When the foul bird releases the disrupting sound, the hosts of Heaven hunt these birds like prey. It is a big deal for the angelic to capture and bring down a foul bird, so nets are often needed in the spiritual realm.

The aim of a foul bird is to bring down the godly shield that the saints have erected by their own release of sound.

We asked, “Are foul birds demonic beings?”

“They are spiritual beings associated with Satan and are outside the will of God.” Mitchell responded.

“Are they essentially a hybrid?” we inquired.

Mitchell explained, “Revelation 18:2[56] describes three different classes. The evil spirits are the lingering human

[56] Revelation 18:2 And he cried mightily with a loud voice, saying, “Babylon the great is fallen, is fallen, and has become a dwelling place of demons, a prison for every foul spirit, and a cage for every unclean and

spirits who are under assignment from a demonic guard. Demons are a separate class, while the foul birds are another class that had not yet been allowed release in the time of Revelation 18:2.

"Remember in the movies *The Lord of the Rings,* where the Uruk-hai came out of the ground? They were a hybrid creation. Foul birds are like that. They are not the same thing, but they are a new class of being like that. Calling them a hybrid creature would be correct because they do not have human DNA, but creature DNA. Nephilim are hybrid humans due to their human DNA, whereas this is a hybrid creature. It is a creature of the physical realm."

The Antidote

Mitchell continued, "Let me talk to you about the antidote. This is the release of angelic forces and the angelic weaponry of nets, chaos nets, and slingshots, together with the voices of the saints in praise and worship, and the voices of the saints in agreement.

"It is both as big and as minute as these things—something minute like a human voice speaking truth, with no lie or manipulation but with heartfelt sincerity. On a massive scale, it is many voices releasing truth as a deterrent to the release of the sound that foul birds

---

hated bird!"

release from their being. These foul birds have been weaponized by Satan and are in league with him."

We asked, "Are they present on the earth now?"

"They are few in number but devastating in effect," Mitchell answered.

"Is this what we have been seeing in some of the national issues and protests of the last several months?" was our next question.

He responded, "Yes. Due to the ruling throne that is present, we have seen the effect of it. It is evidence of a kingdom clash. You are witnessing evil and wicked birds of the air on assignment for Satan. They are to capture the wave frequencies of the air to keep it filled with hate, division, and murder.

Their aim is to stifle or muzzle every other sound.

The atmosphere reflects the kingdom that owns it or is making claim to rule it.

"The shout of God's people, which is the open vocal release of a strong, powerful sound from the lungs of humans in a directed flow of heart, in exaltation of the Father, Jesus, and Holy Spirit, is a shifting force.

Angels need the shout of God's people and their activity to bring down the effects of what foul birds released.

"Foul birds feed on dead things. They ride on the shoulders of men whose hearts have grown cold to Yahweh or any other thing beyond themselves. This includes such things as going after one's own way and the worship of self with freedom from all restraint.

"Do you not call this lawlessness?

Lawlessness is the food that feeds these creatures of the air.

"The birds release more of that, which keeps the wicked cycle going. **The shout of God's people disrupts this cycle.** A bold shout of unison by people who know their God can be weaponized by angels against such beings. It is extremely effective for bringing down foul birds of the air," Mitchell concluded.

Mitchell ended this engagement with this information. Now, coupled with what he taught us and what we learned from James we certainly were more informed about these wicked creatures, but we had more to learn. Once again, we accessed Heaven for instruction. This time, it was Malcolm who had quite a bit to teach us about these foul birds.

Malcolm began, "The foul birds have been defeated by the Kingdom of Glory and by the saints on earth. I can tell you about these things, but you will need to understand one thing. I am talking to you on both sides of the verb tense. I am talking to you about what is, and what will be. Some has not been yet that will be, and some has been that already is. This may be a little difficult to understand, but one way to put it is that it is the working out of all things. This will resolve within the working out of all things."

He continued, "It may seem mysterious to speak of these things, but mysteries have solutions. When the King of Glory brings all things to light, and all darkness that tries to hide will be brought into the light, the saints of God can begin to know the many mysteries of the Father. They will understand from heavenly realms a different dimension of the things which are talked about in Scripture. An enlightenment of the spirit of man is coming by the power of God to be able to reduce the depths of darkness, just as God covered Egypt with such darkness in His judgment of that principality. The Light will begin to infiltrate so many dark places that the dark will lose ground and will be pushed back into its cave. In many ways it is an entity, but it is ultimately ruled over by Yahweh."

He explained, "Your audience will want to hear how to deal with them. For now, it is easiest to work with angels, requesting assistance from the angels of the heavenly host of armies to perform their functions against ruling and reigning spirits that operate through foul birds.

The manifestation of these foul birds is for the purpose of scare tactics to bring fear upon man.

"However, the Father is going to turn the tables on the enemy.

He will use the manifestation of these foul birds for the growing awareness and enlightenment of the ability humans must operate in the unseen realm, and to operate with spiritual power and with the functions of angels to defeat these demonic beings and bring about their exposure.

"A day is coming where these entities will be caught, forced to remain in their physical manifestation, and ridiculed for being the lousy creatures they are. This may be mind-bending to you right now, but I tell you a truth.

It will fall to the sons of God who are operating as children and who follow the leading of the spirit in both power *and* rest. They will work the power of God to the exposure of darkness. They will even force the exposure and capture of the manifestation of beings who feel they have the legitimate right to operate in the unseen without the forcing of the natural. This will be a kingship function and manifestation of the Sons of Glory. For now, the mouths of the saints releases angels to work to capture and pin the wings of these ill-formed creatures causing suffering, and the playing out of demonic forces.

Remind the people that fear within them in any level has no place in this battle, for you will enter the battle with one hand tied behind your back and your feet in shackles if you have agreements with fear within your being.

I speak to you of fear of retribution, fear of reprisal, fear of the unknown, fear of the enemy, fear of the enemy to victory, fear of mystery, fear of humans and what they will say, and fear of man.

"These fears are detrimental to the victory from the mouth of the saint. At this juncture of taking back territory out of the hands of the enemy, *it is necessary to continually check oneself to be sure any fear is eradicated from one's realm.*

"As you begin to speak of these things to people, you must remind them to broaden their understanding, and give themselves permission to see the war from a different viewpoint and in much broader terms than religion has allowed the culture to think, for the war is indeed galactic. Many do not know or understand this yet. One thing I can say to you is that nations are involved. The nations that bow to the Lord Jesus are the nations that become territories of light, outposts of righteousness, and safeguards to galactic realms, for they see and know different realms and realities than you have yet ascertained. Deceived humanity is in league with these dark forces. Do not mistake that nations and individuals are not only deceived, but they have been given over to darkness as well.

As always, the blood of Jesus is the highest substance in all the heavens and on earth.

"That substance is physical and nonphysical, spiritual, and supernatural. The blood of Jesus inside His believers enlivening them is still a mystery to many," he explained.

Chaos and division denote the activity of the foul birds.

Donna kept seeing a picture of humans holding their hands over their ears and running around in circles.

"The foul birds are releasing frequencies which are heinous and detrimental to the natural frame. That is why they were engineered as they were," Malcolm clarified.

Dealing with Them

"Arm angels with chaos nets, bird nets, other types of nets, and slingshots. The nets pin the wings. Pinning the wings has a connection with their mouths; it is almost like when their wings are pinned, their mouth is pinned.

Malcolm continued, "Therefore, loose angels to *pin the wings* of every foul bird and to bring it down out of the atmosphere to the ground. We would refer to this as out of flight mode onto a surface or a grounded station. *Pin the feet* of the birds to the surface to disable their flying ability, *bind their beaks*, and *rip out their tongues*. Eliminating the tongue changes the frequency the bird has. Pinning the wings also stops the frequency emanating from them. The frequency that comes from their wings is used as a detriment against humanity. The pinning of the wings is important; that is why a net is so good. Finally, release angels of light bearing glory.

"Thus, here are a few things to do:

1. Loose angels to pin the wings of the birds.
2. Loose angels to bring them down out of the atmosphere.
3. Pin the feet.
4. Bind the beak.
5. Remove the tongue.
6. Release angels of light bearing glory.

"That is six things which utilize angelic forces for this activity in the unseen realm.

Remember: do not be afraid!

"Notice that angels do not quake. They do not fear. The angels assigned to this type of activity are powerful, focused, and able. On the other hand, currently humanity is incapable of this in all fullness."

As a prayer, do this:

In the name of Jesus,

I loose Fowler Angels to pin the wings of every foul bird and to bring it down out of the atmosphere to the ground.

I authorize them to pin the feet of these birds to the surface.

I authorize them to bind their beaks and rip out their tongues.

I now release angels of light bearing glory.

Recalling an earlier lesson on foul birds, we questioned, "Do we request Fowler Angels (which are angels designed to capture these birds)?"

Malcolm responded, "That is a term you can use. Think of the Fowler as the commander of other angels of light."

Request assistance from the Fowlers.

"Remember, this unseen realm operates with differences that we have not fully grasped," Malcolm explained.

The sense we have is that these Fowlers are on assignment all over the globe and they can come swiftly to our assistance. Fowlers are specialists designed to deal with these evil creatures.

Greater Hunger

There is a greater hunger to know these things now than at any other time in the earth. It is hard for us to understand because we think of the ancient world as much more closely tied to supernatural things. In a way, they were. In a different way, they never saw the illumination of this type of information or did not believe they could overcome it. This was because of the Tree of the Knowledge of Good and Evil at work in humanity, and because of the darkness always seeking to overcome the light by utilizing fear to manipulate and rule. Thus, it was very dark in the sense that those in ancient times were afraid of it.

The Father may also introduce something that He does not fully explain, just as a good parent may gently touch on the basics of a tricky subject regarding the maturity level of a child. As the child grows, the parent is willing to explain more, but still with awareness of the child's ability to comprehend.

Ezekiel's Input

Turning to Ezekiel, we asked, "Ezekiel, do you want to talk to us regarding the metaphor of 'bats in the belfry'?"[57]

His immediate reply was, "'Bats in the belfry' are foul birds. They come to dilute and to bring chaos. I have told you what we (as angels) need, and I told you how to direct angels using chaos nets. You are right to do so in this timeframe.

"Foul birds cause the children of God to *guess* instead of to *know* the Father and be known by Him. It is a distraction, for they operate in distraction. They operate in cancellation—the cancellation of every good intention. They excel in hiddenness and this is often why we (angels) ask you for a flashlight. We have knowledge of their presence and when you collaborate with angels,

---

[57] The term "bats in the belfry" had come to our attention several times recently and Ezekiel confirmed that the "bats in the belfry" and "foul birds" were the same thing.

often our work is to deny these creatures access to realms and regions to which we have boundaries and authority.

"I must caution you," Ezekiel continued, "to be savvy in the things of God, to wear the helmet of salvation, and to know the mind of Christ. Additionally, know that your release of coworking angels is tied to the level of your faith, your belief, your seeing, and your knowledge of the direction Holy Spirit would have you release the activity of angels regarding this."

Ezekiel exclaimed, "We hate these things!

"They work against the minds of human. They often bring clouds and will cloud the mind to create a dullness of mind, so humans lose their mind and reasoning. They bring delusions. They *are* a weapon of darkness. They are *used* as a weapon.

"Ask Holy Spirit to reveal all that is necessary, as the Kingdom has revealed that this is what we are dealing with when we deal with the deluding spirits through the handshake of those working to gain power from realms of darkness. This is part of what is known as 'to deceive even the elect.' It is part of a defeated kingdom, but they are working in dimensional realms too. They are being directed by the agreement of workers of darkness in dimensional places for access to create delusions, a fogginess of mind, cloudiness of thinking, and the presentation of what is not. They often work with the spirit of panic and the spirit of fear—in fact, they cause a spirit of panic. They work to surprise the saint and knock them off balance.

"Let the praise of God be upon the lips of the saints, because the worship of the Father is a weapon, as is the helmet of the salvation of Jesus Christ, co-laboring with angels, and waiting upon the Lord in stillness. These are methods and weapons to become knowledgeable and have a savviness about this. There is still more to be understood," he explained.

Ezekiel continued, "Foul birds are under the direction of the power of the Prince of the Air. They are a sort of go-between between the Prince of the Air and the human operating in league with darkness.

Chapter 23
Miscellaneous Topics

This chapter will cover a variety of topics uncovered during our engagements with Heaven. These were often interactions related to our ministry and things we faced. We share them so you can learn some of the concepts taught by Heaven.

During one such engagement, Ezekiel made it clear that there is one thing he wants to help define for us. That is the fact that, while he often comes and requests particular things which we can request from the Father on His behalf, Heaven continually provisions and re-provisions him as an angel assigned to his rank. He feels this is true for every angel.

"Our increase," Ezekiel said, "comes from your commendation, but it also comes when you request special things for us. Please understand, this does not mean that we always need you to ask on our behalf, because the heavenly Father has well provisioned us for our tasks and what we need. Your spoken requests, or sometimes your suggestions on when to do a thing or what to do (for instance, when you command us to come and put a demon in chains, or to assist you in the unseen with a particular thing)—we are always interested in doing that because this includes us in what you are perceiving from the Spirit of the Lord. It completes a circuit and puts us all in agreement. We are always in agreement with what the Father is saying. Therefore, you do not sense I need very much provisioning today, even though you are wondering, 'Well, I thought you would need it because you have been under all this activity.'" But Ezekiel said, "Where Heaven sees a deficit, Heaven fills it for the angelic ranks. Do not get me wrong. If you were to stop what you have been learning to do, we would notice its lack."

He continued, "We do experience emotions about these things, but our emotions are different than those of humans on God's earth. Our emotions are much more in line with the activity of Heaven and its realms. Remember, I am using language you can understand, but we are aggrieved, or rubbed the wrong way, by humanity's actions sometimes. This has made angels among us go astray and has caused interference within the ranks. However, our purpose in assisting you is always aided when you assist us. This is what we all hope to do to accomplish the work of the Kingdom. It has magnified His glory and the manifestation of His name. Get ready. This will only increase in days ahead. There are some things that are like what was seen in the past, but many things in the future are brand new, with the past providing a launching point for the new.

"I'm going to ask you for a new weapon, mainly because I want you to know that I have this weapon. I call it an intelligent rifle. You might call it a smart gun. It is laser equipped for realms of darkness. It assists us in plunder, in freeing, in taking back territory that has been controlled by darkness (although it never belonged to darkness), and in ensuring the new territory regained stays gained. You can just take this at face value. Some things you don't need to wrap your mind around because there is really no equivalent in your understanding,"

We were also aware that Ezekiel knows exactly what he needs to do, but he enjoys the commission that we give him to go on patrol.

Lydia instructed, "Request of the Father greater wisdom in the use of your communication devices. Be aware that spying and infiltrating through deceptive means is occurring. Pray over the devices, asking angels for help with technology. Know where the Father is at work even now to expose those in your world who are using technology for illegal trades in things like spying, garnering information that is not theirs to garner, and other such activities. Pay attention to other options and areas where these are lessened.

Praying in Tongues

"Praying in tongues is so important," Lydia explained. "Praying in the spirit language is communicating in a code that the devil often cannot decipher because it is of Holy Spirit. It is important and wise to speak this manner of language in your atmosphere consistently and at every prompting of the Spirit of the Lord for you to do so.

"The Spirit of the Lord will prompt you to speak in tongues in advance of things that you cannot yet see, and as a measure of protection for what you will walk into. It is a roadmap for solutions, resolutions, and introducing the solution into the physical realm. It comes through your mouth. If you do not speak in tongues, ask the Lord for this gift.

"He dwells in you and often needs to speak, directing the spirit realm and what it contains in ways that are often mysterious to your understanding."

Angelic Perceptions

Ezekiel had just appeared to us and was unusually brilliant in appearance. Here was the interchange:

"I'll tone it down a little for you," Ezekiel commented.

Donna responded, "I am amazed how you're able to do that, Ezekiel."

He answered, "All angels are able to do this. To speak with humanity, we can do what you call 'dial down' the Glory and do it with ease. Angels want to have relationship with you, and they will do these things to enable that relationship.

"You have requested things on my behalf. The other end of that spectrum is my work from the King of Glory on your behalf. It is a cycle of return that works together. Do not mistake that he is always at war or warring. That would be an incorrect understanding. Just now, you are seeing me relaxed in the realms of Heaven," he finished.

Donna responded, "So, I can meet with you in the realms of Heaven like this, and in the next moment I can see you standing here in my space. I still use the same spiritual eyes, but you are closer now. When you dial it up, I recognize your presence here in my office, like you are standing here at the end of my desk. Then, at some point, you step back into the realms of Heaven, but I can still see you there. It is as though you are standing next to the Help Desk and talking to me. "

"This is how angels come and go into your realm," Ezekiel affirmed.

Speaking to Ezekiel, Donna noted, "You are in a higher estate, but you can always manifest in a lower estate. The cloud of witnesses can do that as well. That is interesting. You are giving me the understanding that it is twofold. We have been talking about stepping into the realms of Heaven, but you are saying that it is really doubled."

He answered, "We are doubled because you can perceive when the realm of Heaven intersects or manifests in the natural. You can see and sense it with spiritual senses. It is the same, but different."

"That is a cool exercise to have your angel come near and then have that angel step into the realms of Heaven," Donna mused. "Then, you step in there to see the same being through Jesus, the door. Whether your spirit is here or in the realms of Heaven, you can engage both ways. You can do it quickly."

Relationship Building

In this engagement a vision of a Rolodex™ [58] appeared. While we were wondering what it meant, Lydia began to explain that the Rolodex represents relationships to our ministry. Some relationships need to end, and other relationships need to be solidified through heavenly trade. Still other relationships need to be guarded and some need to be built. We trade here from Heaven with the Father for the benefit of these relationships, which is that formal network that strengthens. Since relationships are things that angels assist us with, we simply need to request that Ezekiel assist us.

"We are learning about relationships and that you can help us with this. Lydia has been talking about how we do this with you," Donna began.

"I am a relationship arranger. I have access to this Rolodex. I know what is pending to leave, what needs to

[58] A Rolodex™ is a rotating card filing system that was quite popular before the advent of personal computers.

stay, and what needs to be enriched for the ministry to carry out the purpose of the Father as an ambassador of the kingdom," Ezekiel informed us. "I am able to accomplish some rearranging on your behalf, and while I carry this charge out in the background, like Lydia is mentioning, sometimes there will be key times where you'll ask me to perform this duty with specificity."

Lydia spoke up, "You have a moment of opportunity now when you can ask Ezekiel and his team to finalize the order of the relationships that LifeSpring needs to have. This has already begun happening for you as we have worked together, but a new installment of additions, subtractions, and clearing up of some things is needed. That is what we can accomplish together today."

"This is like a commissioning of me," Ezekiel added.

Lydia told us that it is quite simple. We only need to say to Ezekiel, the angel of LifeSpring International Ministries:

> *We commission and charge you to your duty of relationship order and to order relationships for LifeSpring those relationships that will bring benefit of the Father and the blessing of the Father to the ministry.*
>
> *We ask you to circumnavigate the realms and bring these in.*
>
> *We ask you to solidify those in our relationship base with whom the Father is pleased.*

We ask you to transfer out all unnecessary relationships or those relationships causing theft of resources, time, and finances.

We ask you also to clean out debris from those relationships. If the relationship has an ending time in Heavens' scrolls, we request that you abide by the Father's Word in this and bring these relationships to finality and to an end.

We bless those who have walked with the ministry for a time and release them with blessing to their next assignment and season.

We ask Ezekiel to perform the act of sentry at the Gates of the Realm of LifeSpring International Ministries, that no relationships which are not written by the Father or according to divine will be allowed access to the realm either as customer, client, friend, employee, or those aligned as students.

[Take that prayer and customize it to your situation].

Basically, we are asking Ezekiel to swab the decks and to bring into right order the tightened relationships that our Father desires our ministry to have. Clear out the old, bring in the new, and help us establish with solidarity the relationships of people who are already connected to us.

Ezekiel added, "What you're asking me to do is to basically 'spit shine' the relationships at the ministry."

Changing topics, Lydia spoke, "I've come from fresh counsels of the Lord. His counsels are true and full of hope. Do not be greedy but recognize the overwhelming access you have here to trade with the Father, from His realm that is being given in this hour.

"A flow of revelation and understanding coupled with His wisdom, His power, and His might is flowing to earth realm in new and dynamic fashions. The Father desires His sons and daughters in the earth to look up and receive the reign of His beneficial release in this hour. The saints will need this in coming days because all things are becoming new. Unless one has received the new and its accompanying thinking and pathways, one runs the risk of getting caught in old seasons."

In this hour, getting caught in old seasons is not the plan of the Father.

She continued, "He has been releasing teaching to His children and now they must go forward with Him and expand with Him in new revelation. These are revelatory understandings about who He is, who they are, what they exist for. These are new understandings of the perfection of His design and the perfection of His plan. His plan is of ancient ages before time began in the earth realm. Its combination of a marker in an era of time has come and is now."

She continued, "To those who have come near this ministry, hear this:

"Your people are invited to receive abundance and joy, as well as to learn to operate from these things first to enjoy the benefits of the Father as He has purchased you with His Son's own blood. The dynamics of the new era are what you would call rather intense, but Satan's work is like a dam to block up the release of Heaven's flow. That dam will not stand. You simply must put your hand out, touch it and it will dissipate. It is an illusion. Many who do not meditate upon their beds with God lose access to what is being released, because they are not positioning themselves to be a vessel to be filled with it.

"Urge your people to spend time with God. Urge them to give themselves permission to expand beyond the boundaries of their religious training and explore what Yahweh has these days. Be filled with a revelatory flow that will cause you to wonder at its comparison to the trickle you had before now that it has become a fountain and a waterfall. Get under the waterfall. Receive your bounty from your Father. He has no limit. You have not understood this. He has neither limits nor limitations. As King, He accomplishes from His Kingdom realm every desire of His heart.

"Many of your people want to know what God is doing in this hour. They have panicked thoughts and many doubts. They must discipline themselves to put this aside and look up, look beyond, look to the Kingdom of God, look to the realm of the Father, and receive what is being poured out. One of the biggest things that you can help them with in this hour is to learn to receive the new understandings that are coming from Heaven.

"A great many answers to prayer are coming. They will need to be received in a different manner. Some of them will manifest on their own. With others of them, the Father is releasing the answers to His people, but they are not receiving them. This is due to the manner or the newness in which His desire is drawing them to receive. They are trying to remain in old patterns, old thoughts, and deeds, and even relationship and geographical spaces that hinder the receipt of the new flow and ease coming to His people from Heaven.

"In fact, the answers that He is releasing require you to position yourself under an open Heaven to learn, and to receive His direction, instruction, moments, timing, new thoughts, and new thinking. This is going to require you to turn away from the world; not leave the world but turn away from as many distractions as possible. Release to your people the gift of Heaven. Afford them the capacity to see their habits from a new perspective, from a new view, and from a different lens.

"If they will press into that, they will find the motivation to make changes. The flesh lags in this, and often the soul finds comfort in the old, but the new is what the spirit receives and hungers for. This is possible for them in this hour.

"There are many ways that the Father brings these new revelations to help His people make a shift and a change. They come from dreams, visions, knowings, thoughts, signs, wonders, and miracles. By all of them, the Father is bringing His people out from the old and into the new." She reminded us, "Remember how the Father brought the children of Israel out of the slavery of Egypt into the purification process of the wilderness and the promise of the new to cross over into? It is going to be like that."

Bond of Filtering & Bond of Undoing

On this day we engaged Heaven and they were concerned for one of our team members who is a resident of the State of New York. They gave us the following instructions that will be beneficial to you. For this article I will refer to him as Jesse. Here was Heaven's instruction:

"Jesse needs a thing called 'undoing.' It is like quieting. It is an activity of angels.

"Think of where Jesse lives. He is in the state of New York, which is under some principality thrones and some witchcraft, specifically a Jezebel witchcraft spell. The realms of those who carry the Father's light feel the resistance in the spirit realm to their light."

Writ of Undoing

Heaven elaborated, "Undoing is a work of angelic hosts to undo spells of witchcraft. When you become aware of witchcraft activity through human agents and the voices of those aligned with darkness, angels can be requested to operate. You can request this as an amendment to a court case and you can also appear in the Court of Angels to request a Writ of Undoing. It is easier for angels to operate undoing through paperwork that comes from other court cases and you can request of the Father that the angels carry out this Writ of Undoing."

"Do not play with this one," Heaven warned. "This is not something to be done on a whim. This is something to be done only when you have been told to and when you are assured that witchcraft is in play. The human soul cannot lead you to the accuracy of this discernment. You will need to discern it by the spirit.

Bond of Undoing

"If you see witchcraft bonds in the Bond Registry, you can request a godly Bond of Undoing. It is a bond at that point. Requesting this bond on the Bond Registry releases the paperwork to angels to carry out the undoing. It is immensely powerful. You can use it as a defense item and as often as necessary but let me be clear with you—**do not** guess at this!" Heaven cautioned.

Bond of Filtering

"I want to tell you about another bond, which is called the Bond of Filtering," Heaven continued. "This bond also releases powerful paperwork to angels on behalf of the individual. A Bond of Filtering it is going to help your physical atmosphere so that your spirit is more able to discern spiritual things. You may have to work with this one for a while to realize how it works. A Bond of Filtering is for the purpose of angelic activity in that person's atmosphere to cause discernment and revelation to be at a higher level. It enables the atmosphere to carry spiritual discernment and spiritual knowing at a higher upgraded level.

Working in Tandem

"These bonds are often found together or are good to use together because they can work in tandem. When you have been told that there is witchcraft at play, you need the Bond of Undoing. You can also subsequently ask for the Bond of Filtering as that causes a filtering in the spirit that angels are helping with so that the human spirit is catching, grasping, and knowing, so that they become more aware of what is going on. A mature saint operating under the Bond of Filtering is then enabled and empowered to be their spiritual self with their spirit forward and to operate from that route from the Father's realm. This may also help with their dreaming during their night seasons."

With one more question, our engagement was over. "This is when you expose the enemy's work so that you can employ the use of the angelic host?" we inquired.

"Yes," was Heaven's reply with no further explanation.

We have learned that if Heaven does not explain to you that day, they probably will soon. Just keep listening for it.

May this understanding broaden your work in the realms of Heaven as we see captives set free!

. . . . .

Being Rescued

Ezekiel had one more thought to share, "Thank Jesus that a person willing to remove themselves from the kingdom of darkness has but to cry to Jesus and ask him to rescue them. The words, 'Jesus, I need you to rescue me and save me,' are the words angels hearken to bring human bloodlines and human minds out from realms of darkness. We hearken to these words quickly, and we like them. We are designed to hear these words. Calling upon the name of Jesus begins the process of this."

Chapter 24
Engaging Trust

Donna and I had checked in with the Finance Department regarding the ministry and we met with George, a Man in white who serves as our financial advisor. We asked if we need to watch for anything concerning the ministry. His reply was to watch for theft. He reminded us of John 10:10 where Jesus tells the listeners that the thief comes to steal, kill, and destroy. That is his job description. He does not behave any other way.

George reminded us, "Regarding anywhere that you *feel* stolen from, learn to count on that as probably meaning that you have, indeed, been stolen from. You can always appear in the Court of Reclamations to request to know what you may receive back, and *you may also ask for more than what has been stolen from you.*"

We asked him to expound on that a bit and he replied with, "You know the scripture that says, 'You have not because you ask not'?[59] Then you ask of the Father and the enemy comes and does his work to steal. Heaven says you can ask for more. The Bible calls this abundance. Ask for more than you can think. You must get beyond natural accounting. You want to engage with heavenly accounting. You want to engage with spirit accounting. You want to engage with the accounting of the King's release for all assignments.

Every assignment is fully funded.

He advised us, "You can ask for those assignments that we are working on—that we are engaged with. You can ask for abundance of Heaven to supply, support, and overwhelmingly fund the assignment: for the CourtsNet assignment, for the book writing assignments, for the release of teaching. This is the one we should talk about most."

The Release of the Teaching

George continued, "Sometimes you come and ask me if your giving quotient is good. I usually tell you that, yes, you are within range. One of the main reasons I tell you this is because of your release of the heavenly teaching in the books, and in the Tuesday trainings, and in the Facilitator Training. This is where I am talking about heavenly accounting. You have got to look at it as

[59] James 4:2-3

heavenly accounting. It is reaching the eyes, ears, and minds of many more people than you think it is. It is being discussed, it is being pondered, and it is even being prayed about. People are reading this and asking the Father about this.

"Do you see that all of this is the trade? All these things are the trade that comes from the initial release of your insight from Heaven as a ministry. This is the ministry assignment: to shepherd the sheep in such a way that they grow to maturity through overcoming every obstacle.

It is not that the sheep are protected from every obstacle, but it is that they overcome every obstacle which grows them to maturity.

"If every assignment is fully funded by the King and the Royal Kingdom of which you are a part, then anywhere you feel stolen from, you can appear in court to request an abundance to come back to you.

The thing you must be careful of is doubt.

"The enemy is hunting for a thought of doubt which gives them access to thieve more widely.

"Become convinced in your mind, as you are engaged in the assignment before you, that our Father in Heaven is supplying every need.

Engage your trust for abundance.

"This is the tweak where (earthly) accounting and Heavenly accounting differs, because however much you can trust for is the amount that is released."

Donna intoned, "George, you did not say it is the amount you can believe for; you said it is the amount you can trust for."

George said, "Many believe, but you must trust. Which is greater, believing or trusting? That is an interesting distinction. I trust the Father.

Trust is an equation of one's relationship with the Godhead.

"A small relationship equals small trust. A damaged relationship—damaged trust.

"Where agreement with the lies or the inability to receive is present, then you will have shortage of trust.

"Receiving abundance is linked to trusting the Father for that abundance, for that prosperity," George explained. "Many are needing to verbally trust Him for more. After they first request for more, then comes trust. As Heaven gets closer to earth, trusting God will become easier. Trusting God when it is hard brings Heaven closer to earth. It is the work of the spirit within the human. Everybody needs encouragement about trust. Don't they?"

Donna asked, "George, are you aware of areas where we have been stolen from that have not come to our attention yet?"

He replied, "We still have on the books:

"The outstanding amount of technology,[60] theft of time, theft and the weariness that produced. It is a taxation on your emotions—your confidence."

If you began to look at all these things as substances that are being stolen from you, you will begin to ask the Father to make the enemy pay back. We have not because we asked not.

Go to the Court of Reclamations where:

The Court of Reclamations is going to tell us what we have ready to be returned.

The Court of Accounting is going to cause a looking into a matter and cause a settlement to be made.

George explained, "Both work hand in hand, but work separately as well. This is true for the individual, not just for a grouping. Think of it like this: you have

---

[60] We had recently experienced a catastrophic failure of a primary computer's hard drive that caused a good deal of challenges for our team.

ministry spheres that have been stolen from you, you have individuals within spheres being stolen from, and you have cities, nations, and people groups that are being stolen from."

Suddenly Donna could see the Accounting Department. "I am requesting an accounting of that which has been stolen from me and I am requesting of my Father an abundance of return from the substance of which I have been robbed," she requested. Then, we let Heaven's Accounting Department go to work on our behalf.

George continued, "When you request for the substance of what you have been robbed of you do not even have to know what the substance is, you just need to show up and ask.

"This is the journey."

Chapter 25

What Has Been Stolen from You?

During one encounter, Lydia advised us, "Ask Holy Spirit, 'Where have I been stolen from?' Heaven is in a good mood to give back what has been taken from the saints. Often, you have been stolen from due to broken walls which correlate to bloodline iniquities. Once you have worked through the bloodline iniquities, you can engage Heaven regarding theft from your realm and your destiny." Thus, we began another engagement.

She continued, "Where do you feel you have been stolen from? When Satan stole from *you,* he *also stole* from the Kingdom of Heaven. You need to regain a certain degree of outrage towards the enemy at his thievery. Understand that what you perceive is that the enemy has taken from the Kingdom itself. It gives Heaven great pleasure to return to the saints what has been stolen.

Stolen in Previous Generations

"This includes what has been stolen in previous generations. Many saints do not ask for what was stolen from their ancestry, thinking only of the current generation or their current life. However, Yahweh is always in the mood to release what was taken from previous generations.

Appear in the Courts of Heaven
to ask what can be reclaimed
in the Court of Reclamations.

"Do not just appear there once but keep coming back," Lydia instructed. "This Court of Reclamations is one that gives both counsel and adjudication regarding many losses experienced by many generations."

Be the One!

Be the one in your bloodline to begin the restoration of all things. You will have great pleasure in doing this. Many live in a state of lack because it is a condition that has passed down through the generations. Be the one in your bloodline to reverse the curse. Utilize the Court of Reclamations to bring adjudication for your bloodline of the many things that still impact it. This is not just wealth; this includes creative flows, salvations, new books, and new scrolls—anything that was blocked by iniquity or sin. As an individual's bloodline is cleansed and purified by the blood of Jesus, you can have hope in the ability to stand righteously in the Court of Reclamations to receive an unlocking of what was blocked.

Many things have been blocked by current events, so avail yourself of the Court of Reclamations. Let it not be said in Heaven that you did not come to ask. This is the joy for which the Lord died upon the cross.

Get It ALL Back!

There is a way to get it all back, but many have not tried to through the courts. They have attempted to do so through petitions and supplications, but they have not appeared in court.

Ask the counsel of the court.

What might you ask for from the Court, whether large or small?

Here is a hint: remember that you do not know all things. Therefore, how could you possibly know what to ask for in the court? Wait upon the counsel of Holy Spirit and the counsel of the court, as all things are done in perfect timing.

Due to of the goodness and grace of God and what is coming, if you do not appear in the Court of Reclamations to begin the process, you can never receive what is meant to come back to you.

Desensitized to Loss

You may have become desensitized to loss. The theft of Satan has existed for so long on the earth that humanity has coped or put up with it, and in some measure, has accepted their loss. This was never the plan of the Father. You have no idea how timely this is.

Ask Holy Spirit to give you the grace NOT to be desensitized to the loss when you have access to the courts to make the enemy pay it back.

Envision piles of gold as well as piles of herbs and plants and growing things.

Envision piles of transportation-oriented things.

Envision piles of calendars, clocks, and stop-watches.

Envision piles of what can be described as fountains.

Envision butterfly nets, fishing nets, and harvesting nets.

These are the things waiting to be claimed through the work of the courts.

Have fun!

Chapter 26

Drawing a Bridge

Let me help you make a connection or draw a bridge between two things: (1) the work you do for the cleansing of the bloodline which includes repentance for profane worship, gaining freedom slavery issues, dealing with idolatry issues, rebellion in the bloodline, serving other gods, going after strange fire, and things of this nature and, (2) the work of reclamation of things lost or stolen to you or your generations. The bridge that connects is called hope. What you will experience as you deal with one area is that you will cross into the Court of Reclamation. You will be able to receive what was stolen from your bloodline, whether overtly or covertly, or even through the ignorance of previous generations. This is the hope.

There are far more resources of Heaven that need to be released into the earth than have even been asked for at this point.

Many reading this have not completed the work of redeeming their bloodline from profane worship, idolatry, and rebellion. This must be the first step before continuing. It is necessary to work with Holy Spirit and ask Him to show you the areas of your bloodline that require repentance so that theft can then be addressed.

Envision a pile of title deeds and books. The books represent words that Satan comes to steal so that you do not make changes in the earth realm. He thinks he has plundered and captured a bounty. Get your words back! Get your message back!

You have a choice whether or not to follow through with this teaching and take hold of it like a bulldog with a bone, not letting go until you have received from the Judge everything that you have been given by the Father. There is a protocol and a timing for this, but there is also the beginning of a new flow for the people of God. The remnant who walks through this, utilizing the blood of Jesus to cover their sins in agreement with their own repentance and confession will begin to shift the earth realm. This is very needed in the current day.

Even the number of salvations that come into the Kingdom on a yearly basis are linked with those who go to the court to cleanse their bloodlines.

When believers begin to operate in the Court of Reclamation to receive from the Just Judge that which was stolen from them, including members of their future and present bloodlines, these individuals will be saved by Holy Spirit's operation in their lives. These cleansing works and work in the Court of Reclamation are linked, and they are important to recognize.

The early church knew this. They were in a dispensation to recognize the authority of the Kingdom. They understood what we do not today, which is that when a victorious King is triumphant, He is the ultimate ruler over many things, and His word is the final word. Their grasp of this has been lost in the present day, but that understanding can return.

Complacency in a Bloodline

When there is complacency in a bloodline, that bloodline has been robbed of their right to know God through Jesus. They have this right because they are created beings. The will and plan of God is for that bloodline to know Him, not religiously, but intimately. The bottom line is that the expansive prayers of courtroom work and standing in court for the repentance of a bloodline reaches many. It delves deep into DNA levels that would largely rock our understanding and enables the freedom of Holy Spirit to then move on to many related DNAs. This gives a new definition to evangelism, doesn't it? It is evangelism from your secret place because they are meant to know both the pleasure of their Creator and the pleasure that their

Creator has. They are meant to know the truth, and the will of God is that they would have it.

Chapter 27

Becoming a Revelation Receiver

It was during yet another meeting with Heaven when Lydia spoke, "Envision a chess board where the King of kings has won the game and you get to remind the enemy that the match has already been won. It is a check mate, for God's Kingdom reigns supreme over every lesser kingdom, and every deity pretending to call itself God. However, the need for the saints to recognize their role as children of God to agree with His will in the earth realm so that the plans of God can continue to unfold in planet earth and cause it to triumph in full measure and in every area with finality and completeness is great is crucial. The plans the Father has for His church, as well as the plans He has for His people, and the fact that He must announce the greatness of who He is to the earth, are all present.

The children of God are engaged in the working out of these plans.

These plans include freeing captives (those held in captivity to spiritual bondages) and these plans are also linked to their freedom through God's sons and daughters. We get to participate!

"Confrontation with the world and its systems and structures is unavoidable, but do not be frightened, weak, or feel vulnerable to the systems of this world because the greater Kingdom is coming closer, and as it approaches in closer dimensions, the enemy is more wrathful, and the battle is more easily seen," Lydia continued. "This plays into the purposes and plans of the godhead and even of the church. The ecclesias of the earth are beginning to see the warfare more clearly. *This should not frighten you; this should enlighten you* to your part and your place, even your position in Christ Jesus as overcomers. You have already secured the triumph.

"New revelation of God's people's role and position in this victory is being released. You must have awareness of the war in spiritual places and allow it to motivate you to your position and role as a son of God, one who operates in assurance of the Father's business, His activity, and His plan.

"Many things are being uncovered to your sight. Even now, do not let the uncovering of evil frighten you.

Have no agreement with fear.

"Allow the work with the angels of God as they uncover the bold contradictions of the enemy's lies and shenanigans to cause your spirit to rejoice because you have knowledge of the one who overcomes all in seeking God for knowledge.

Request angelic activity to work with the words of your mouth as you release this knowledge into different realms.

"This refers to angelic realms, human realms, physical plane realms, and spiritual realms. The sons and daughters of God are beginning to see who they really are. They are beginning to know the triumphant power of God that dwells richly within them as they release it verbally, as they do this without religious thought but as a family member of God's family, born again through the blood and cross of Jesus.

"As you do this, your mind begins to shift to authority, and you begin to see with wider acceptance your own ability of agreement and alignment with the godhead to enforce the victory of Jesus.

"Surely this is a calling up of the armies of the church, and here I do not mean the angelic armies—I mean the armies of God's children who sometimes war, and sometimes release the angels to war, and sometimes operate in more kingly dispensations of the release of a Word of God. Please know this," Lydia implored. "Angels are on assignment to hear what the saints are saying.

Please understand the words of the saints must match the words of the Father for angels to go to work.

"I am talking about what you have as written word, but I am also talking about what you have as supernatural word, the rhema word, the breath of Yahweh. I also mean the spirit leading your ears and eyes to know that an unfolding needs to happen, and the Father has decided, of His will, that He will work with His sons and daughters in the earth so that His will would be done in the earth," she concluded.

Revelation Helps Thwart the Enemy

We asked Lydia, "How does this work out against the plans of the enemy?"

She responded, "You can supernaturally understand the plans of the enemy so that you can circumvent them. After all, are you not from a more powerful kingdom?

Revelation sometimes appears to your sight as to what the plans of wickedness would accomplish for the express purpose of you bringing about the plans of God in that circumstance.

"You have learned this must be done in numerous ways: court cases, declarations, agreements, and verbal releasing of that agreement, so that the angelic activity around you hearkens to that word.

Releasing Rhemas

"The Word of God—and I am not talking about scriptures but talking about rhema[61]—

The Word of God released from your tongue Is exactly what angels listen for and they go to work.

"This was the powerful moment of the amazement of Jesus when He talked to the Centurion because He saw the Centurion understood.

What is in the unseen spiritual realm can be seen, known, heard, picked up, and understood by God's children maturing as they will. Some choose not to mature.

"Heaven has no issue with that because Heaven trusts the Spirit to do His work of revelation, so that your minds

[61] Rhema is the Greek word describing a word that has become alive to you.

can begin to understand the role of the saved in the earth realm.

"For too many seasons, the church—and I do not mean church like you would define it in the past, I mean the praying ecclesias—have been shy of their true authority and ability.

Remember, there is great power in where two or more agree and touch upon the same thing, asking of the Father to release His power to that thing.

"Many in your day are awakening to this and must continue to awaken to it.

"Not only do we have Scribe Angels, which have been sent out into the earth to record the words of the saints as they verbally release the Word of God, but there are other angels who have been released to *prompt the saints to release the Word of God,*" Lydia explained. "Many among you are leaders in this while some are just coming into it.

What must be understood is the work of darkness to cloak the verbal words of God's saints.

"Words are warfare. They end wars, begin wars, and settle wars. It has always been a clash of kingdoms.

However, from our viewpoint, this clash of kingdoms is only to grow up the saints to reveal to them their true position in Christ and the overcoming victory of His kingdom." she clarified.

Becoming a Revelation Receiver

Be encouraged that new revelation can come to those who ask, seek, and hunger as if a starved man at a banquet for the revelation that Yahweh wants them to release over their spheres of influence.

Remember, each sphere of influence has a boundary as apportioned to them by God.

Are you filling up your boundary with the words of God?

Are you asking angels to assist you in the receipt of revelation?

Do you know the revelatory Word of God over a circumstance in your sphere?

Some of this is plainly evidenced in scripture. The Lord has not left us unknowing, but in our day—in our current calendar on earth—we must receive the Word of the Lord by revelation, by dreams and visions, and by understanding all of this through the lens of the goodness of God. He wants to grow up His children. His plan is for the righteousness within His children to be seen. The people who are listening to this ministry are seeking to be these mouths in the earth. Some, if not most, are hidden in private and do this in their prayer work, which causes Heaven to rejoice.

"An army has been mobilized among God's people and any who desire to join shall do so simply by faith—through what they release as the revelatory Word of God, not agreeing with the presentation of world structures, but agreeing with truth through the Spirit of Truth and through the opening of the ear. That is the work of angels in this area," Lydia explained. "Is it not great fun?

"I am using the word *fun* to refer to when you see the outcome of a contended timeline as it settles through the verbal release of the ecclesia in agreement with the will and purposes of God. Is it not a moment of joy where you see this take place through agreements within the Body of Christ on earth?

Your Common Goal

Unity and a sense of oneness comes from laboring together for common goals.

"Let your common goal be what is written in scripture and what is revealed to you. Make room for different expressions of the same goals of heavenly places and give room to those among you who are empowered by the Spirit to fulfill their mission in this hour. Your great joy comes from this as you see enemy plots exposed and defeated. Do not worry about the timeframe. Leave the timing of it to the heavenly realm—to the unseen realm and the activity of the angels. Believe me, they are at work," Lydia advised. "You are going to be able to sense their work in greater measure in future days. Let this cause your heart to rejoice."

She continued, "It is possible to rejoice in advance of the manifestation of the result in the 3-D realm. Your spirit knows how to do this. **Give permission to your spirit to come forth and rejoice in the victory of the Lord in all circumstances.** This will preserve your soul and keep it from weariness.

Focus on the things of the Lord.

"Divide out—and you can request angels to help you with this—and discern the frequencies of the Lord and the activities of angels versus that of darkness. Your spirit can help you do this.

The Power of Silence

"Let me give you a reminder of how powerful your words truly are," Lydia continued. "Be mindful to steward and shepherd over your words well—not from the soulish realm as some do, but from your spirit. Silence—and what I mean by that is what we call holding our tongue or not making an expression of sound—is as important as what you agree with vocally. Silence is a symbol of disagreement.

What you do not vocalize is equally important as what you do vocalize.

"It is as if I give you permission not to say anything. You will see this in scripture where it is told of Jesus who as the lamb before the slaughter, He did not open His mouth.[62] This is a sign of trusting the Lord. Some try to battle verbally with other humans when the skirmish is not in the natural plane, it is in the unseen plane. You must address this plane before the natural plane can align to carry the weight of the truth you must release.

"Are these not good mysteries?" Lydia asked us.

"I encourage you that this is just some of the foundational things we as children of God get to be reminded of.

A Symbol of Strategy

Lydia continued, "Remember, I started this by talking about a chess board. The chess board is a symbol of strategy. You need to recall how strategic (this is the word you use) your Father in Heaven truly is. He is so strategic that He laughs from His throne at the antics of a defeated kingdom for He has won His children back to

---

[62] Isaiah 53:7, Matthew 17:27

Himself by His own son and the blood that He shed. He is not worried, and He has great plans for earth's realm even still.

Rejoice!

"Worship is rejoicing, so set your mind to rejoicing. The battle has an outcome of victory, but the strategies in play as on a chess board sometimes are not seen until the final move. I share this symbol with you that you may know you are involved in a strategic time and that YOU are strategic," she clarified. "Your position is strategic to what the Father is doing as you learn who you are and begin to rest in the truth of what He is calling each person to do. Personal assignments, even small ones, are great in His sight.

Work with the Angels

"Work with the angels of God, receive their messages. Some of these messages will be brought in dreams. Some will be brought in knowings. Begin to trust this. However, I will say this. The work of this ministry to lead bloodlines in the cleansing of iniquities is linked with and important to one's ability to hear the Word of God, see what the plans of the Father are, as opposed to the plans of the enemy and follow with verbal release and co-laboring with the activity of angels," Lydia concluded.

Cleansing of Bloodlines

Next, Ezekiel (who had appeared) began, "This work of your ministry is still foundational. Learn to come quickly to the courts so cases may be ruled upon on their behalf, so legal grounds are removed from enemy plots. The cleansing of bloodline iniquities for this reason is still important. As you continue the work of gaining the courtroom verdicts on your behalf to purge and cleanse iniquities, the enemy is upset to no longer have access to your realm with wrong frequencies. Thus, deluding spirits and lying spirits have a more difficult time twisting, blinding, and duping you. This is why you have felt the importance of emphasizing the cleansing of the bloodlines, as you have been taught."

Cooperating with Messenger Angels

"At present, there are many Messenger Angels that have been released to the saints of God, many more than you can imagine," Ezekiel spoke. "Commission me to work with these Messenger Angels to connect with those in your sphere of influence. The activity right now of Messenger Angels globally is highly active and these Messenger Angels often need assistance from and the protection of other angels as they carry out their duty.

"It is like in wartime, where the lines of communication between generals behind the lines is not the active fighting, but these communication lines must be guarded. Therefore, we offer the following prayer:

Father, we just request in the name of Jesus that these Messenger Angels be given assistance by Ezekiel, his ranks, and commanders, and we asked for backup help for Ezekiel for this? We thank you and commission you to work to protect the Messenger Angels so that they take their communication to the saints so, that no message is lost. We commission you to that in Jesus' name.

"Many of these messengers are being released in the night hours—when you are just drifting to sleep, when you first awake, or they may show up in your dreams," Ezekiel explained. "That seems to be the types of messages that are coming right now that Heaven is talking about. Then the messages, once received, play out during the daylight hours."

Heaven wants to help us understand this, to help us say:

I receive the messages of the Messenger Angels into my realms and into my understanding. I receive the messages. I trust them. And I believe them. They are going to make a difference in the lives of people and in the purpose of God for the planet, and for the purpose of God for the nations. I receive the Messenger Angels who have messages from God that will change the nations. I agree to receive them.

Commission the angels assigned to you to work with Ezekiel, his commanders, and his ranks, as their alignment with the ministry gives us permission to work with your angels. “Sometimes,” Ezekiel added, “We stir up their angels or we enlist them as we work together.”

Knowing

“The sons of God are learning to see spiritually, and their discernment is improving. These things go hand in hand with knowing who you truly are and how valuable your words are to enact the plans of God.

“One of our activities,” Ezekiel pointed out, “is to cause the right word to go to the right ear. We do this often and we often overcome the wrong word to the wrong ear and the wrong word to the right ear.”

Protecting Your Ears

Ezekiel continued, “Envision an angel with a sword who sees a wrong word as an object that is traveling in a dimension of space. The angel sees that this word is headed for an ear that should not hear it, so he takes his sword and deflects the word as it goes by, or he may chop it asunder. Therefore, the wrong word does not enter that individual’s ear—I am talking about your spirit ear *and* your natural ear. You need angels to help you that your spirit ear and your natural ear do not hear the wrong word—the word that brings doubt, the word that brings fear, the word that brings the activity of iniquity, the word that brings curses, or the word that brings works of darkness.”

Angels love their activity of doing this. It is important to agree with one's angels that they are at work doing this well. This is what I mean when the angels of this ministry desire to work with the personal angels assigned to you. They team up together in the spirit realm to better bring down the wrong word. Ezekiel remarked, "Trust me, in this hour, you need our help."

We asked, "Is there a commissioning concerning this?"

"It is always good to commission your personal angels to deflect the wrong words from your ears," he responded.

Remember, you have two sets of ears.

Commission your angels to deflect and bring asunder wrong words that would enter your physical ear and your spiritual ear. This is remarkably like wrong sight.

Protecting Your Eyes

Wrong visuals can enter your spirit eyes and your physical eyes; therefore, you need angels helping you on both.

Protecting Your Heart

After the ears and eyes, there is a matter of the heart.

Remember, what your heart longs for is proof of what your ears have heard, and your eyes have seen.

Thus, you are cautioned to focus on the Lord, joyful worship, and gratefulness. Repeating the Words of God enables this, but the work of in the unseen realm is equally important. Commission your personal angels to cut asunder wrong words, declaring that they will not enter your realms, nor will they intersect your pathways, but that you will see and hear guidance from Heaven.

Angels do this equally. They see to the releasing into your sight, and ears, and heart the goodness of the Father, His plans, and His purposes.

What angels cannot do is make agreement for you.

That is your role. Choose wisely what you will agree with.

"I have not even spoken to you about the element of time for all messages have time elements attached to them. This is true from the kingdom of darkness because it is also true of the Kingdom of Light and has only been stolen and corrupted by the copying of the kingdom of darkness, but do not worry. Angels will see to their task in the unseen and employ their abilities to do what you cannot do. For this reason, they have been assigned to you, even created so that they accomplish things for you," Ezekiel concluded.

Chapter 28
Epilogue

A great deal of activity is occurring in the earth at this time, but even more is occurring in the spirit realm. Heaven is never outdone by Hell's schemes, so whatever you see, hear, or face is not the end. An already-defeated foe has refused to read the memo that he has lost.

As you have read through these chapters, we trust you have been blessed, broadened, challenged, and matured to be more of the Son the Father envisioned. The late Kim Clement had a saying he would often repeat in his meetings:

> *You're somewhere in the future and you look much better than you look right now!*

He was right. You are somewhere in the future and you do look much better. Once you partake of revelation, you can never be the same. That is a good thing. Never go back to how you were. Always press forward. Always expand. Always live spirit-forward!

Let me close with this recent engagement with Lydia. It was quite encouraging.

"What is your recommendation for those reading this book?" we inquired.

She responded, "Savor the goodness of God. Savor the goodness of the Father. Savor the goodness of the Son.

"Savor means to mull in the mouth. To savor is to agree with the goodness of God, to hold it within you, to bring it close, and to embrace it."

Lydia continued, "Many today need peace, which comes from savoring the goodness of the Father. Many have troubled hearts, and a heart tuned to savor the things of Yahweh translates the peace of His kingdom through each of the realms of your being. Let His peace rule in your spirit realm, soul realm, and body realm. From this peace, you enter a flow with a spirit-forward manner of living in your life and begin reaching the markers of your destiny. Chaos is sent against the people of God to keep them inward-focused rather than Heaven-focused."

Savoring the Spirit of God and His Goodness.

Continuing, Lydia said, "Savoring, with the spirit of God, the Father's goodness assists you in leaving the world behind, even though you are amid the world. Savoring the Father's goodness means learning to appreciate His aroma, His taste, His feel, and His strength. This is what Obed Edom did in the scriptures when the Ark of God's presence was at his house. The fruit that you see mentioned there was the result of the presence of God being savored and appreciated. Know that the presence of Yahweh will have its own effect on each of your realms and even on your outlook on life. Your many cares will seem to fade as you savor the goodness of God.

"Combine the elements of His communion table in remembrance of covenant so that your realms are more perfectly sealed, and your mind is focused on Him because of tuning the flow of your heart toward His goodness. In all things, give thanks and determine to love the Lord your God with all your heart, soul, mind, and being, Invite Him into and all your realms and into every nuance.

"It is true. Many of you speak of feeling tumultuous times. This is the current reality, but the soul gets weary. The spirit of your being, however, can be the captain of your ship as you weather the height of the waves and the tumultuous coming days. Look with your eyes to a new day. Noah had to get used to a new position after the flood waters receded. He was unfamiliar with this new ground and stance, and grace was given to him to come out of the ark and embrace the new.

"This is now the work of the saints to embrace with gratefulness—the new that is being ushered in by Yahweh. The tumultuous times do not last forever; the new will come. Begin now to advance your territory by embracing it and the unknown future with the assurance that God is good. Begin now to verbally direct your life with your mouth by saying:

> *God is good in my future. I am not alone in my future. I am better in my future than I am in my present because the Word of God says I will go from glory to glory.*

"Just say right now,

> *I am going to go from glory to glory and my future is better than my present. I agree with this word.*

"It will be so new that people will have to find their stance in it when it arrives, but it will be good. It will be rich, with coming pockets of richness on the earth."

Lydia stated, "I will not define the word rich for you. It falls to you, the sons of God on the earth, to discover the richness of Yahweh in your present day. Let hope arise and look with hope to your future! A new ability is coming to embrace others, to enjoy their expressions and to watch with amazement what God frees them from and how he delivers them.

"It is as if a veil is being removed and your hearts will be softened to one another to view each other as God's beloved children, no matter where each comes from. This will begin in the church. This will not be found where the spirit of religion rules rigidly over the saint with a domination that refuses to let them go. In coming days, even the spirit of religion will let go. It will not be everywhere, but it will be noticeable where Jesus, the

King of Glory, has vanquished that spirit of religion. It will be exposed as a trifling and, as scripture points out, will show that religion lacks power from Yahweh. People will be able to see that it holds no power, nor the King's Glory, and will begin to recognize this in large degree.

"Not everyone is locked under religion, but those who are will be afraid. However, it will be, as it has always been, a choice to come out and be free, just as the children of Israel crossed out of Egypt. It will be a similar event, where God's children will choose to come out from under the rule and dominion of religion into a vibrant awareness of their ability to chase after the things of God and to apprehend them. You will see much repentance as this erupts on the face of the planet as well.

"This will not be without a response from darkness, but nevertheless, Jesus has overcome the world.

"Remind your audience that, in Jesus, they are more than they think they are, and His love for all His children spreads far and wide, higher and deeper; and is more than you can imagine or think.

"Receive agape[63] daily and the grace that accompanies it to move through your time. Repent as often as needed as the Spirit of the Lord uncovers a thing to your heart; simply repent. Request that the covenant blood blessings of Yahweh flow abundantly to you and to your family. An increase is coming on earth that cannot be limited in its design. Some will call it abundance.

---

[63] Agape is the divine love of the Father for everyone.

Some will call it reaping. You can know this is the pleasure of God for His people. I urge you to announce in agreement with Him:

Let it begin. Let it begin. Let it begin!"

Appendix

Learning to Live Spirit First

A challenge with how we were taught about the Christian life is that everything was put off until sometime in the future. Then, we read the letters of Paul and we experienced a disconnect. Heaven, to us, was a destination, not a resource. We knew nothing about learning to live from our spirits. We only knew what we had been doing all our lives, since birth, and that is to live to satisfy our soul or our flesh. We sorely need to learn an alternative way of living.

Exchanging Your Way of Living

Paul recorded these words in his letter to the Romans:

> *Those who are motivated by the flesh only pursue what benefits themselves. But those who live by the impulses of the Holy Spirit are motivated to pursue spiritual realities. (Romans 8:5)*

We must learn to live spirit first! We must exchange our way of living. We must learn to live from our spirit. We need to understand the hierarchy within us:

- We are a spirit.
- We possess a soul.
- We live in body.

Each component has a specific purpose in our lives. Our spirit is the interface with the supernatural realm. It is designed for interfacing with Heaven & the Kingdom realm. Your spirit has been in existence in your body since your conception. Your soul has a different purpose. It communicates to your intellect and your physical body what your spirit has obtained from Heaven. It is the interface with your body. Your body houses the two components and will follow the dictates of whichever component is dominating,

Most of us have never been taught about having our spirit dominate. Rather, we have merely assumed that our soul being dominant was the required mode of operation.

Our soul always wants to be in charge. Our soul is susceptible to carnal or fleshly desires, lusts, and behaviors. It will, at times, resist our spirit and body. It must be made to submit to your spirit by an act of your will.

Your will is a means of instructing either component (spirit, soul, or body) what to do. Your soul has a will and so does your spirit. You choose who dominates!

Your body, on the other hand, has appetites that will control you in subjection to your soul. They become partners in crime—remember that second piece of chocolate cake it wanted? Your body will try, along with your soul, to dictate your behavior. It will likely resist the spirit's domination of your life. However, it will obey your spirit's domination if instructed, and your body can aid your spirit if trained to do so.

The typical expression that operates in most people's lives is that their soul is first, body second, and their spirit is somewhere in the distance in last place.

In some people, especially those very conscious of their physical fitness or physical appearance, there is a different lineup. Their body is their priority, the soul second, and again their spirit is the lowest priority.

Heaven's desire for us is vastly different. Heaven desires that we live spirit first, soul second, and body third. Since we are spiritual beings, this is the optimal arrangement. For most of us, our spirit was not activated in our life in any measure until we became born again.

If, after our salvation experience, we began to pursue our relationship with the Father, then we became much more aware of our spirit and learning to live more spirit conscious. The apostle Paul wrote in his various epistles about living in the spirit or walking in the spirit. Because we are spiritual beings, our spirits cry out for a deepening of relationship with the Father. Our spirit longs for it and will try to steer us in that direction.

Our soul has certain characteristics that explain its behavior in our life. This is the briefest of lists, but I think you will get the idea. Our soul is selfish. It wants what it wants when it wants it. It can be very pouty. It can act like a small child. It is offendable and often even looks for opportunities to be offended. Our soul is also rude.

Our body has a different set of characteristics. It is inconsiderate, demanding, lazy, and self-serving. It does not want to get out of bed in the morning, for many people. In others, it wants to be fed things that are not beneficial.

However, characteristics of our spirit are hugely different. If we live out of our spirit, we will find that we are loving and prone to be gentle. We desire peace. We are considerate. We are far more contented when living out of our spirit. Also, joy will often have great expression in our lives.

Sometimes we have experienced traumas that create a situation of our soul not trusting our spirit. The soul blames the spirit for not protecting it. The irony is that typically, our soul never gave place to the spirit so that it could protect us. The soul places false blame on the spirit and it must be coerced to forgive the spirit. Then the soul must relinquish control to the spirit. Once the soul forgives the spirit, the two components can begin to work in harmony.

If I were to flash an image of some delicious, freshly cooked donuts in front of you, what would happen? For many, their body would announce a craving for one. What if, instead, I showed you an image of a bowl of broccoli? How many people would get excited about that? Probably not as much excitement over a bowl of broccoli would be exhibited. Which does your body prefer—the donuts or the broccoli? For the untamed soul, the donuts are likely to win out every time. Which do most kids prefer?

In any case, you can train yourself to go for the healthier option. A principle regarding this that I heard years ago is summed up like this:

What you feed will live—
what you starve will die

What do we want to be dominant—our spirit, our soul, or our body? The part we feed is the part that will dominate.

For some, they feed their soul and live by the logic of their mind. Everything must be reasoned out in their mind before they will accept it. However, because our soul gains its insight from the Tree of the Knowledge of Good and Evil, it will always have faulty and limited understandings.

How do we change this soul-dominant or body-dominant pattern? We instruct our soul to back up and we call our spirit to come forward. Some people may need to physically stand up and speak to your soul and say, "Soul, back up," and as they say those words, take a physical step backward. Then, speak to their spirit out loud and say, "Spirit, come forward." As you speak those words, take a physical step forward. This prophetic act helps trigger a shift within them.

Live spirit first!

Benefits of Living Spirit First

Why would you want to live spirit first? Let me present several reasons to you. Living spirit first will create in you an increased awareness of Heaven and the realms of Heaven. It will create a deeper comprehension of the presence of Holy Spirit, and of angels and men and women in white linen. You will be able to better hear the voice of Heaven. You will experience greater creativity, productivity, hope, and peace. You will become more aware of the needs of people that you can meet.

As you live spirit first, you will be able to access the riches of Heaven in your life. Petty things that formerly bothered you will dissipate in importance or impact in your life. You will be able to move ahead, not concerning yourself with the petty, mundane, or unproductive things that have affected your life before you began to live spirit first.

This way of life is more than a game changer—for the believer, it is the only way to live. You will face challenges as you build your business or live your life from Heaven down, but you will more readily be able to access the solutions of Heaven as you live with an awareness of the richness of Heaven and all that is available to you as a son or daughter of the Lord Most High. I encourage you, do not live dominated by your soul. *Live spirit first!*

Works Cited

MerriamWebster.com/swing. (2021, January 21). Retrieved from Merriam-Webster: https://www.merriam-webster.com/dictionary/swing?src=search-dict-box

The Greek Old Testament (Septuagint). (2021, January 18). Retrieved from Ellopos.net: https://www.ellopos.net/elpenor/greek-texts/septuagint/chapter.asp?book=38&page=3

Description

Receiving Riches from Heaven

"A change of season is fast approaching. A new revelatory flow is going to appear, and I am letting you know so you will be aware of the change," Heaven says. "Nevertheless, continue what you are doing, stepping into, and expanding in.

"What you are creating with the Father will expand people's understanding and give them a surfboard to surf on the wave of God that is coming into the earth for the people of God, those whom He has called.

"They will need a surfboard to stand upon to surf the new wave of God that is coming. It is the new wave of the membership of the body; the new wave of a divine remembering of who the Bride really is and what she is here to do. It is a new wave of coping with what the enemy stirs up, and even releases from Counsels of Darkness, that is already overcome by the overcomers in Jesus."

Heaven said these words to me recently and this book is a compilation of some of the things Heaven shared. Step in and be refreshed by what Heaven has to say.

About the Author

Dr. Ron Horner is a communicator and author of several bestsellers He writes and teaches on the Courts of Heaven as well as how to engage Heaven and how to live from Heaven down. He has written over 20 books. His work has taken him around the globe.

Ron is the founder of LifeSpring International Ministries, which serves to advocate for individuals and businesses in the Courts of Heaven. He teaches a weekly Mentoring Group on the Courts of Heaven primarily and conducts seminars regularly. He is also founder of Business Advocate Services, a worldwide consulting company (BASGlobal.net).

Other Books by Dr. Ron M. Horner

Building Your Business from Heaven Down

Building Your Business from Heaven Down 2.0

Cooperating with The Glory

Engaging Angels in the Realms of Heaven

Engaging the Mercy Court of Heaven

Four Keys to Dismantling Accusations

Engaging the Courts of Heaven

Engaging the Help Desk of the Courts of Heaven

Engaging the Courts for Ownership & Order

Engaging the Courts of Healing & the Healing Garden

Engaging the Courts for Revelation – Volume 1

Engaging the Courts for Your City *(Paperback, Leader's Guide & Workbook)*

Freedom from Mithraism

Releasing Bonds from the Courts of Heaven

The Courts of Heaven Process Charts

Overcoming Verdicts from the Courts of Hell

Overcoming the False Verdicts of Freemasonry

Unlocking Spiritual Seeing

Cooperating with The Glory

Lingering Human Spirits

Let's Get it Right!

Revelation Brings Revolution

"A change of season is fast approaching. A new revelatory flow is going to appear, and I am letting you know so you will be aware of the change," Heaven says. "Nevertheless, continue what you are doing, stepping into, and expanding in.

"What you are creating with the Father will expand people's understanding and give them a surfboard to surf on the wave of God that is coming into the earth for the people of God, those whom He has called.

"They will need a surfboard to stand upon to surf the new wave of God that is coming. It is the new wave of the membership of the body; the new wave of a divine remembering of who the Bride really is and what she is here to do. It is a new wave of coping with what the enemy stirs up, and even releases from Counsels of Darkness, that is already overcome by the overcomers in Jesus."

Heaven said these words to me recently and this book is a compilation of some of the things Heaven shared. Step in and be refreshed by what Heaven has to say.

Dr. Ron Horner is a communicator and author of twenty books on the subjects of the Courts of Heaven and engaging the realms of Heaven. He teaches through weekly classes, a training program, seminars, and conferences.

Ron is the founder of LifeSpring International Ministries, which serves to advocate for both individuals and businesses in the Courts of Heaven. He is also the founder of Business Advocate Services, a worldwide consulting company (BASGlobal.net).

LIFESPRING PUBLISHING
LIFESPRINGPUBLISHING.COM